defining new moon

defining new moon

Vocabulary Workbook for Unlocking the *SAT, ACT®, GED®, and SSAT®

Brian Leaf, M.A.

WILEY

Wiley Publishing, Inc.

Library of Congress Cataloging-in-Publication Data:
Leaf, Brian.
  Defining new moon : vocabulary workbook for unlocking the SAT, ACT, GED, and SSAT / Brian Leaf.
    p. cm.
  ISBN-13: 978-0-470-53299-7
  ISBN-10: 0-470-53299-8
1. Vocabulary tests--Study guides. 2. Vocabulary--Study and teaching (Secondary)
3. Educational tests and measurements--Study guides. I. Title. II. Title: Vocabulary workbook for unlocking the SAT, ACT, GED, and SSAT.
  PE1449.L28 2009
  428.1'076--dc22
                              2009034458

Printed in the United States of America

10   9   8   7   6   5   4   3   2   1

Book production by Wiley Publishing, Inc., Composition Services

Acknowledgments

Thanks to Stephenie Meyer for her storytelling and her terrific vocabulary. Thanks to my agent Linda Roghaar and my fantastic editors at Wiley, Greg Tubach and Carol Pogoni. Thanks to Amy Sell, Malati Chavali, and Adrienne Fontaine at Wiley for getting the word out. Thanks to Pam Weber-Leaf for great editing tips, Zach Nelson for sage marketing advice, Ian Curtis for assiduous proofreading, Manny and Susan Leaf for everything, and of course, thanks most of all to Gwen and Noah for love, support, and inspiration.

Table of Contents

About the Author

Brian Leaf, M.A., is the author of *Defining Twilight* and the four-book SAT and ACT test-prep series *McGraw-Hill's Top 50 Skills*. He is Director of the New Leaf Learning Center in Massachusetts, and has provided SAT, ACT, GED, SSAT, and GRE preparation to thousands of students throughout the United States. Brian also works with the Georgetown University Office of Undergraduate Admissions as an alumni interviewer, and is a certified yoga instructor and avid meditator. For more information, visit his Web site at www.brianleaf.com.

How to Use This Book

This workbook contains 40 groups of vocabulary words selected from *New Moon*. Many of these words will show up on your SAT, ACT, GED, or SSAT. Beginning at Group 1, refer to the *New Moon* page where each vocabulary word appears. Read the word in context and come up with a definition. Then check your definitions against those provided in this workbook and make corrections. I'll also show you synonyms, word parts, and memorization tools. Read these over a few times, and then complete the drills. Do that for all 40 groups. There's no easier or more fun way to learn 600 vocabulary words! By the end of this book, your vocabulary will be larger, your test scores will be higher, and you'll be a *New Moon* scholar!

Group 1

Callous Prophecy

Find each of the following words on the *New Moon* page number provided. Based on the way each word is used in the book, guess at its definition.

1. **Callous** (p. 1) might mean _____

   _____

2. **Relentless** (p. 1) might mean _____

   _____

3. **Inexorably** (p. 1) might mean _____

   _____

4. **Extraordinarily** (p. 2) might mean _____

   _____

5. **Toll** (p. 2) might mean _____

   _____

6. **Wizened** (p. 4) might mean _____

   _____

7. **Prophetic** (p. 6) might mean _____

   _____

8. **Quantifiable** (p. 7) might mean _____

   _____

Let's see how you did. Check your answers, write the exact definitions, and reread the sentence in *New Moon* where each word appears. Then complete the drills on the next page.

Definitions

1. **Callous** (p. 1) means *insensitive*. On page 1 of *New Moon*, the crowd is **insensitively** in Bella's way as she rushes to prevent Edward from sparkling like a diamond in the middle of the plaza. The word *callous* actually comes from the dead **insensitive** skin of a callus that you might get after a tough field hockey or basketball season.

2. **Relentless** (p. 1) means *endless* or *constant*. *Relent* means *end*, and *-less* means *without*, so *relentless* and *endless* mean *without end*. Synonyms: ceaseless, eternal, incessant, interminable, perpetual, unremitting.

3. **Inexorably** (p. 1) means *unstoppably*. This is a serious high-level vocabulary word—don't you love that your SAT, ACT, GED, or SSAT score will go up just from reading the *Twilight* saga?!

4. **Extraordinarily** (p. 2) means *very*. This is a great word to break apart. *Extra-* means *beyond*, like *extrasensory* (beyond normal senses), *extracurricular* (beyond the normal curriculum), and *extraterrestrial* (beyond the Earth, like E.T.). So *extraordinarily* means *beyond ordinary*.

5. **Toll** (p. 2) in this case is a cool word for *the ring of a bell*, as in Ernest Hemingway's novel, *For Whom the Bell **Tolls.***

6. **Wizened** (p. 4) means *wrinkled*. As people age, they become **wiser** . . . and they get **wrinkles,** so there you have it.

7. **Prophetic** (p. 6) means *predicting something*, like *prophets* do in the Bible. For all you *Twilight* diehards (Twihards), on this page we learn that Bella's birthday is September 13. Synonyms: prescient, visionary. *Prescient* is an interesting word to break apart. *Pre-* means *before*, as in *preview*, *preregister*, and *pretest;* and *-scient* refers to *know*, as in *science* and *sentient* (aware). So *prescient* means to *know beforehand—to predict!*

8. **Quantifiable** (p. 7) means *measurable*. In fact, *quant-* refers to *number*, as in *quantity*, and the Spanish word *cuanto*.

Synonyms: Select the word or phrase whose meaning is closest to the word in capital letters.

1. CALLOUS
   A. extraordinary
   B. insensitive
   C. tolling
   D. playful
   E. generous

2. RELENTLESS
   A. wizened
   B. temporary
   C. extracurricular
   D. impermanent
   E. endless

3. INEXORABLY
   A. all-present
   B. visionary
   C. prescient
   D. unstoppably
   E. relaxed

4. PROPHETIC
   A. visionary
   B. quantifiable
   C. extraordinary
   D. ceaseless
   E. extraterrestrial

Analogies: Select the answer choice that best completes the meaning of the sentence.

5. Callous is to insensitive as
   A. wizened is to tall
   B. extraordinary is to simple
   C. quantifiable is to limitless
   D. prophetic is to visionary
   E. relentless is to timid

6. Incessant is to constant as
   A. prescient is to prophetic
   B. kind is to callous
   C. quantifiable is to detested
   D. extrasensory is to immortal
   E. toll is to vampire

Sentence Completions: Choose the word that, when inserted in the sentence, <u>best</u> fits the meaning of the sentence as a whole.

7. The team progressed _____ toward the goal; the defense could do nothing to stop them from scoring.
   A. quantifiably
   B. wisely
   C. inexorably
   D. extraordinarily
   E. prophetically

8. The wizened sage was known for her _____ visions; villagers came from all over seeking her predictions and advice.
   A. relentless
   B. prophetic
   C. incessant
   D. wrinkled
   E. false

1. **B.** *Callous* means *insensitive. Extraordinary* means *beyond ordinary,* and *tolling* means *ringing.*

2. **E.** *Relentless* means *endless.* Use the process of elimination—cross out all choices that are **definitely** wrong. *Wizened* means *wrinkled, extracurricular* means *beyond the normal curriculum,* and *impermanent* means *not permanent.* Notice that *im-* means *not,* which is why *impermanent* means *not permanent.*

3. **D.** *Inexorably* means *unstoppably. Visionary* and *prescient* mean *predicting.*

4. **A.** *Prophetic* means *visionary. Ceaseless* means *endless.*

5. **D.** Make a sentence with the two words. Ideally, define the first word using the second. For example, "A callous person is insensitive." Then, try your sentence for each pair of words in the answer choices.

   A. A wizened (wrinkled) person is tall . . . no, not necessarily.
   B. An extraordinary (beyond ordinary) person is simple . . . no.
   C. A quantifiable (countable) person is limitless . . . no, that makes no sense.
   (D.) A prophetic person is visionary . . . yes!
   E. A relentless person is timid . . . no, a relentless person never gives up and is not shy.

6. **A.** "Incessant means constant."

   (A.) Prescient means prophetic . . . yes, they both mean *predicting.*
   B. Kind means callous (insensitive) . . . no, they are opposites.
   C. Quantifiable (countable) means detested (hated) . . . no, they are totally unrelated.
   D. Extrasensory means immortal . . . no. An immortal like Edward, Alice, or Jasper might have extrasensory abilities, but the words are not synonyms.
   E. Toll means vampire . . . no, *ringing a bell* and *vampire* are unrelated, well . . . except to Edward, Bella, and the Volturi at the Palazzo dei Priori.

7. **C.** Think of a word to fill the blank. Often you can borrow a word right out of the sentence.

   > "The team progressed _unstoppably_ toward the goal; the defense could do nothing to stop them from scoring."

   Then use the process of elimination, crossing off answer choices that **definitely** do not work, and see which answer choice fits best. *Inexorably* means *unstoppably* and is the best answer.

8. **B.** "The wizened sage was known for her _predictive_ visions; villagers came from all over seeking her predictions and advice."

   When trying to come up with a word to fill the blank, always look for evidence in the sentence—"seeking her predictions" tells you what you need to know.

Impasse

Find each of the following words on the *New Moon* page number provided. Based on the way each word is used in the book, guess at its definition.

1. **Impending** (p. 7) might mean _____

   _____

2. **Tribute** (p. 7) might mean _____

   _____

3. **Tawny** (p. 8) might mean _____

   _____

4. **Mimic** (p. 9) might mean _____

   _____

5. **Articulation** (p. 9) might mean _____

   _____

6. **Impasse** (p. 10) might mean _____

   _____

7. **Glum** (p. 12) might mean _____

   _____

8. **Prominent** (p. 12) might mean _____

   _____

6 Let's see how you did. Check your answers, write the exact definitions, and reread the sentence in *New Moon* where each word appears. Then complete the drills on the next page.

1. **Impending** (p. 7) means *looming* or *about to happen.* Synonym: imminent.

2. **Tribute** (p. 7) means *something that honors.* The movie *Across the Universe* was a **tribute** to the Beatles. Synonyms: homage, paean.

3. **Tawny** (p. 8) means *yellowish-brown.* We see lots of great vocab words in *New Moon* for Edward's yellowish-brown eyes: *ocher, topaz,* and of course *golden.*

4. **Mimic** (p. 9) means *imitate.* This word comes from the word *mime*—the guy from your second-grade birthday party who pretended to be trapped in an imaginary box while **imitating** a monkey. Synonym: ape.

5. **Articulation** (p. 9) means *clear pronunciation.* The word even has a bunch of distinct and **clearly pronounced** syllables. I love how English works—oftentimes you can tell what a word means just by the way it sounds.

6. **Impasse** (p. 10) means *dead end.* In Group 1, you learned that *im-* means *not.* You can**not pass** through an **impasse.** Synonyms: deadlock, stalemate.

7. **Glum** (p. 12) means *sad.* I don't want to give anything away, but you better get used to this word; lotsa glum and **sad** words are coming in this story, at least for a while. Synonyms: despondent (very glum), gloomy, morose, pessimistic, sullen.

8. **Prominent** (p. 12) means *noticeable* or *important. New Moon* Quiz 1: Who are the three most **prominent** vampires in the vampire world? (Discuss your answer with your friends.)

Synonyms: Select the word or phrase whose meaning is closest to the word in capital letters.

1. IMPENDING
   A. important
   B. imminent
   C. relentless
   D. disturbing
   E. callous

2. TAWNY
   A. ocher
   B. burgundy
   C. pale gray
   D. reddish-brown
   E. black

3. IMPASSE
   A. toll
   B. prophecy
   C. articulation
   D. stalemate
   E. tribute

4. PROMINENT
   A. articulate
   B. glum
   C. noticeable
   D. morose
   E. sullen

Analogies: Select the answer choice that best completes the meaning of the sentence.

5. Tribute is to homage as
   A. tawny is to mimic
   B. ape is to paean
   C. impasse is to deadlock
   D. despondent is to excited
   E. prominent is to impending

6. Prominent is to hidden as
   A. callous is to considerate
   B. relentless is to incessant
   C. wizened is to wrinkled
   D. prophetic is to prescient
   E. impending is to imminent

Sentence Completions: Choose the word that, when inserted in the sentence, best fits the meaning of the sentence as a whole.

7. Mrs. Nicholas announced that a quiz was _____, so the students began studying immediately.
   A. tawny
   B. prominent
   C. wizened
   D. visionary
   E. imminent

8. Negotiations were at a(n) _____, so delegates from both countries were sent to break the deadlock.
   A. tribute
   B. impasse
   C. mimicry
   D. prominence
   E. articulation

1. **B.** *Impending* and *imminent* mean *about to happen.* In the drills from here on, I'll review words from previous Groups to help you understand and memorize them. *Relentless* means *endless,* and *callous* means *insensitive.*

2. **A.** *Tawny* means *yellowish-brown.* If you chose choice B, *burgundy* (deep red), shame on you, Alice is not like that!

3. **D.** *Impasse* and *stalemate* mean *dead end. Toll* means *ring a bell, prophecy* is a *prediction, articulation* means *clear pronunciation,* and *tribute* means *something that honors.*

4. **C.** *Prominent* means *noticeable. Articulate* means *able to speak (and pronounce words) clearly. Glum, morose,* and *sullen* all mean *sad.*

5. **C.** Make a sentence with the two words. For example, "Tribute is a synonym of homage." Then, try your sentence for each pair of words.

   A. Tawny (yellowish-brown) is a synonym of mimic (imitate) . . . no.

   B. Ape (imitate) is a synonym of paean (tribute) . . . no.

   C. Impasse (deadlock) is a synonym of deadlock . . . yes!

   D. Despondent (very sad) is a synonym of excited . . . no, they are opposites.

   E. Prominent (noticeable) is a synonym of impending (about to happen) . . . no.

6. **A.** "Prominent (noticeable) is the opposite of hidden."

   A. Callous (insensitive) is the opposite of considerate . . . yes!

   B. Relentless (endless) is the opposite of incessant (endless) . . . no.

   C. Wizened (wrinkled) is the opposite of wrinkled . . . no.

   D. Prophetic (predicting) is the opposite of prescient (predicting) . . . no.

   E. Impending is the opposite of imminent . . . no, they both mean *about to happen.*

7. **E.** Think of a word to fill the blank, selecting a word directly from the sentence when possible, and then see which answer choice fits best.

   "Mrs. Nicholas announced that a quiz was *immediate,* so the students began studying immediately."

   Imminent means *about to happen* and fits best.

8. **B.** "Negotiations were at a(n) *deadlock,* so delegates from both countries were sent to break the deadlock."

   Choice B, *impasse,* means *deadlock* and works best.

Contingency Plan

Find each of the following words on the *New Moon* page number provided. Based on the way each word is used in the book, guess at its definition.

1. **Microscopic** (p. 13) might mean _____

   _____

2. **Uncanny** (p. 13) might mean _____

   _____

3. **Reciprocate** (p. 13) might mean _____

   _____

4. **Ostracism** (p. 14) might mean _____

   _____

5. **Trivial** (p. 16) might mean _____

   _____

6. **Fickle** (p. 17) might mean _____

   _____

7. **Contingency** (p. 18) might mean _____

   _____

8. **Sadistic** (p. 18) might mean _____

   _____

10 Let's see how you did. Check your answers, write the exact definitions, and reread the sentence in *New Moon* where each word appears. Then complete the drills on the next page.

1. **Microscopic** (p. 13) means *very small*. *Micro-* means *small,* as in the Game Boy micro, which is a newer and **more compact** Game Boy handheld game console. Incidentally, *nano-,* as in the iPod nano media player, means *very, very small.*

2. **Uncanny** (p. 13) means *strange and remarkable.* It can be a synonym for *extraordinary,* meaning *beyond the ordinary* (remember that *extra-* means *beyond),* from Group 1.

3. **Reciprocate** (p. 13) means *give back.* The prefix *re-* means *again* or *in return,* which makes sense, like you're giving a gift in return for one given to you. Synonym: requite.

4. **Ostracism** (p. 14) means *being excluded.* Even if you didn't know this word, you can figure it out in context. Several lines earlier, Bella tells you that her friends sit on one side of an invisible line at the lunch table and the Cullens sit on the other side. So "this minor ostracism" refers to **being excluded**—on the other side of the invisible line.

5. **Trivial** (p. 16) means *unimportant.* But, sometimes this word is used in a humorous way—Edward's "razor-sharp, venom-coated teeth" being near Bella is definitely not trivial.

6. **Fickle** (p. 17) means *unreliable* or *changing too easily.* Romeo was in love with Rosaline but then quickly fell for Juliet, so Edward calls him fickle. Synonyms: capricious, erratic, impulsive, mercurial, vacillating.

7. **Contingency** (p. 18) means *possibility,* and a *contingency plan* is a *plan for a possible outcome.* Synonym: eventuality.

8. **Sadistic** (p. 18) means *intentionally cruel.* This word actually comes from the name of the Marquis de **Sade,** who is known for some pretty freaky and disturbing activities. The opposite of a *sadist* is a *masochist,* one who likes to <u>experience</u> rather than <u>inflict</u> pain. The sadistic vampire that Bella is referring to is, of course, James.

Synonyms: Select the word or phrase whose meaning is closest to the word in capital letters.

1. RECIPROCATE
   A. reapply
   B. mimic
   C. ape
   D. requite
   E. pronounce

2. OSTRACIZE
   A. articulate
   B. sadistic
   C. exclude
   D. relent
   E. cease

3. TRIVIAL
   A. vacillating
   B. capricious
   C. erratic
   D. insignificant
   E. chatty

4. FICKLE
   A. microscopic
   B. uncanny
   C. mercurial
   D. inconsequential
   E. sadistic

Analogies: Select the answer choice that best completes the meaning of the sentence.

5. Callous is to sadistic as
   A. trivial is to tawny
   B. extraordinary is to unusual
   C. sadistic is to masochistic
   D. contingency is to eventuality
   E. glum is to despondent

6. Uncanny is to extraordinary as
   A. fickle is to mercurial
   B. erratic is to microscopic
   C. ostracism is to impasse
   D. tawny is to blue
   E. impending is to morose

Sentence Completions: Choose the word or words that, when inserted in the sentence, best fits the meaning of the sentence as a whole.

7. Sierra felt that the administration saw her concerns as _____, callously ignoring what she viewed as imminent danger.
   A. uncanny
   B. capricious
   C. trivial
   D. sadistic
   E. imminent

8. Qasim always plans for the _____ of rain; he knows that even with sunny skies, rain in Forks is a(n) _____ possibility.
   A. toll .. impending
   B. eventuality .. mimicking
   C. articulation .. tawny
   D. tribute .. microscopic
   E. contingency .. imminent

1. **D.** *Reciprocate* and *requite* mean *give back*. *Mimic* and *ape* mean imitate.

2. **C.** *Ostracize* means *exclude*. You might *ostracize* a *sadistic* (cruel) person, but the correct synonym should more directly define the word. *Articulate* means *well spoken,* and *relent* and *cease* mean *end*.

3. **D.** *Trivial* and *insignificant* mean *unimportant*. *In-* means *not,* so *insignificant* means *not significant—unimportant*. *Vacillating, capricious,* and *erratic* mean *unreliable*.

4. **C.** *Fickle* and *mercurial* mean *unreliable* or *changing too easily*.

5. **E.** "Callous (insensitive) is less extreme than sadistic (cruel)." The SSAT loves this kind of setup: "_____ is less extreme than _____."
   A. Trivial (unimportant) is less extreme than tawny (yellowish-brown) . . . no.
   B. Extraordinary is less extreme than unusual . . . no.
   C. Sadistic is less extreme than masochistic . . . no.
   D. Contingency is less extreme than eventuality . . . no, they both mean *possibility*.
   (E.) Glum is less extreme than despondent (very glum) . . . yes!

6. **A.** "Uncanny means the same thing as extraordinary."
   (A.) Fickle means the same thing as mercurial . . . yes, they both mean *unpredictable*.
   B. Erratic (unpredictable) means the same thing as microscopic (very small) . . . no.
   C. Ostracism (exclusion) means the same thing as impasse (dead end) . . . no.
   D. Tawny (yellowish-brown) means the same thing as blue . . . no way.
   E. Impending (about to happen) means the same thing as morose (glum) . . . no.

7. **C.** "Sierra felt that the administration saw her concerns as *ignorable,* callously ignoring what she viewed as imminent danger."
   Look for evidence in the sentence and choose a word to fill the blank. You want a word for *ignorable*. Then use the process of elimination. *Trivial* means *unimportant* and fits best.

8. **E.** "Qasim always plans for the looming *possibility* of rain; he knows that even with sunny skies, rain in Forks is a(n) *looming* possibility."
   Think of a word to fill each blank and use the process of elimination for one blank and then the other. Only cross out choices that **definitely** do not fit. If a word could work or if you're not sure, leave it. *Contingency* means *possibility,* and *imminent* means *looming*.

Blanched Trio

Find each of the following words on the *New Moon* page number provided. Based on the way each word is used in the book, guess at its definition.

1. **Remote** (p. 19) might mean _____

   _____

2. **Mayhem** (p. 20) might mean _____

   _____

3. **Trio** (p. 20) might mean _____

   _____

4. **Reverie** (p. 20) might mean _____

   _____

5. **Moot** (p. 20) might mean _____

   _____

6. **Ceasing** (p. 20) might mean _____

   _____

7. **Blanched** (p. 20) might mean _____

   _____

8. **Convalescence** (p. 22) might mean _____

   _____

Let's see how you did. Check your answers, write the exact definitions, and reread the sentence in *New Moon* where each word appears. Then complete the drills on the next page.

1. **Remote** (p. 19) means *far away*. Let's practice using the context to figure out what this word means. "His eyes still <u>remote</u>" refers back to Bella's description of Edward as ". . . focused on something <u>far away</u>." The SAT, ACT, GED, and SSAT always use this setup, too—you can figure out the meaning of a vocabulary word from the words and sentences around it!

2. **Mayhem** (p. 20) means *disorder*. Synonyms: anarchy, bedlam, chaos, pandemonium, turmoil. *Mayhem* actually comes from the word *maim* (to permanently injure) and often implies *violent disorder*.

3. **Trio** (p. 20) means *a group of three*. The prefix *tri-* refers to *three*, as in *tricycle* (a bike with three wheels), *triangle* (a shape with three sides), and *triumvirate* (a group of three people, or Volturi vampires in this case, holding power).

4. **Reverie** (p. 20) means *thoughts* or *daydreaming*. That's easy to remember since *reverie* sounds like *reviewing*, which is pretty much what it is—in her mind, Bella is reviewing the paintings that she saw in Carlisle's study.

5. **Moot** (p. 20) in this case means *irrelevant*. It can also mean *uncertain*. I love this word. I could say it all day: "Moot!"

6. **Ceasing** (p. 20) means *stopping*. You saw the word *ceaseless*, meaning ***not*** *stopping*, as a synonym for *relentless* in Group 1.

7. **Blanched** (p. 20) means *paled* or *turned white*. Notice how often Bella turns white in these books—perhaps a prediction for things to come. . . . The word *blanch* looks like the Spanish word *blanco* and the French word *blanc*, which mean *white*. When you notice an English word that reminds you of a Spanish or French word, usually they are related. You can frequently use Spanish, French, Latin, German, and other foreign-language words to feel out the definition of a new word.

8. **Convalescence** (p. 22) means *recovery*. Synonym: recuperation.

Synonyms: Select the word or phrase whose meaning is closest to the word in capital letters.

1. REMOTE
   A. chaos
   B. turmoil
   C. bedlam
   D. anarchy
   E. far away

2. MAYHEM
   A. pandemonium
   B. triumvirate
   C. ostracism
   D. prominence
   E. impending

3. CEASING
   A. turning white
   B. requiting
   C. relenting
   D. reciprocating
   E. tolling

4. CONVALESCE
   A. become ill
   B. quantify
   C. recuperate
   D. ostracize
   E. blanch

Analogies: Select the answer choice that best completes the meaning of the sentence.

5. Blanching is to white as
   A. trivializing is to important
   B. reverie is to convalescing
   C. mimicking is to articulated
   D. quantifying is to inexorable
   E. convalescing is to healed

6. Remote is to near as
   A. trio is to quartet
   B. reverie is to thoughts
   C. anarchy is to order
   D. moot is to uncertain
   E. fickle is to capricious

Sentence Completions: Choose the word or words that, when inserted in the sentence, best fits the meaning of the sentence as a whole.

7. The governor warned that if the tax was levied on the colonists, _____ and possibly rebellion would ensue and all laws aimed at keeping order would be _____.
   A. mayhem .. reciprocated
   B. anarchy .. contingent
   C. reverie .. trivial
   D. chaos .. moot
   E. sadism .. extraordinary

8. Julius Caesar led the famous Roman First Triumvirate and conquered distant lands stretching far north into _____ areas of Gaul and Britain.
   A. remote
   B. blanched
   C. ostracized
   D. uncanny
   E. prominent

1. **E.** *Remote* means *far away. Chaos, turmoil, bedlam,* and *anarchy* mean *disorder.*

2. **A.** *Mayhem* and *pandemonium* mean *disorder. Triumvirate* is a *group of three leaders, ostracism* is *excluding someone, prominence* means *fame or importance,* and *impending* means *about to happen.*

3. **C.** *Ceasing* and *relenting* mean *ending. Requiting* and *reciprocating* mean *giving back,* and *tolling* means *ringing a bell.*

4. **C.** *Convalesce* and *recuperate* mean *heal.* Make sure you try all of the choices. Don't just get to an answer that reminds you of the word and stop. Choice A, *become ill,* is a related word. But, *convalesce* means *recover from illness,* not *become ill,* so choice C is the best answer. Always try all choices and use the process of elimination to find the **best** answer.

5. **E.** "Blanching makes something white."
   A. Trivializing makes something important . . . no, trivializing makes something unimportant.
   B. Reverie (daydreaming) makes something convalescing (healing) . . . no.
   C. Mimicking (imitating) makes something articulated (clearly pronounced) . . . no.
   D. Quantifying (counting) makes something inexorable (unstoppable) . . . no.
   (E.) Convalescing (healing) makes something healed . . . yes!

6. **C.** "Remote (far away) is the opposite of near."
   A. Trio (group of three) is the opposite of quartet (group of four) . . . no, they are different, but not opposites.
   B. Reverie is the opposite of thoughts . . . no, they are synonyms.
   (C.) Anarchy (disorder) is the opposite of order . . . yes.
   D. Moot is the opposite of uncertain . . . no, *moot* can mean *uncertain.*
   E. Fickle is the opposite of capricious . . . no, they both mean *unreliable.*

7. **D.** "The governor warned that if the tax was levied on the colonists, *rebellion* and possibly rebellion would ensue and all laws aimed at keeping order would be *lost.*"
   If there is a word, such as *levied* (imposed), that you don't know in the question, cross it out and try filling the blanks without it. Usually you don't need any one specific word to get a question correct! The SAT designs it that way. *Chaos* means *disorder,* and *moot* means *meaningless.*

8. **A.** "Julius Caesar led the famous Roman First Triumvirate and conquered distant lands stretching far north into *distant* areas of Gaul and Britain."
   Choice A, *remote,* means *far away* and works best.

Ravenous Vampires

Find each of the following words on the *New Moon* page number provided. Based on the way each word is used in the book, guess at its definition.

1. **Obscure** (p. 23) might mean _____

_____

2. **Chafing** (p. 23) might mean _____

_____

3. **Prehistoric** (p. 23) might mean _____

_____

4. **Virtuously** (p. 23) might mean _____

_____

5. **Furtively** (p. 24) might mean _____

_____

6. **Aversion** (p. 26) might mean _____

_____

7. **Basilisk** (p. 28) might mean _____

_____

8. **Ravenous** (p. 29) might mean _____

_____

Let's see how you did. Check your answers, write the exact definitions, and reread the sentence in *New Moon* where each word appears. Then complete the drills on the next page.

1. **Obscure** (p. 23) means *unclear* or *difficult to understand.* Synonyms: abstruse (puzzling), recondite.

2. **Chafing** (p. 23) means *becoming annoyed or irritated.* One time my brother ran a marathon and his sweaty shirt **chafed** his nipples; they were so **irritated** that he had to wear Band-Aids for a week!

3. **Prehistoric** (p. 23) means *very, very old.* Pre- means *before,* so *prehistoric* means *before history—very, very old.* Bella's Chevy is from 1959, pretty darn old for a truck.

4. **Virtuously** (p. 23) means *with goodness or honor. Virtuously* literally means *with virtue (goodness).* Synonyms for *virtue:* rectitude, righteousness.

5. **Furtively** (p. 24) means *secretly.* These words are used a lot in the *Twilight* saga—there's got to be a fair bit of secrecy when mythical creatures live among us. Synonyms: clandestinely, covertly, stealthily, surreptitiously.

6. **Aversion** (p. 26) in this case means *avoidance.* It can also mean *intense dislike,* but the context on page 26 in *New Moon* tells you that it means *avoidance:* "Jasper smiled, too, but kept his distance." The SAT, ACT, GED, and SSAT love to use a word with several meanings and ask you to determine its meaning in the context. Synonyms: animosity, antipathy, disinclination, enmity.

7. **Basilisk** (p. 28) refers to *a legendary giant serpent with a deadly stare.* Okay, you might not have gotten all of that from the context in *New Moon,* but you probably knew that it referred to a pretty nasty stare.

8. **Ravenous** (p. 29) means *very hungry.* Synonyms: famished, gluttonous, insatiable, rapacious, voracious.

Synonyms: Select the word or phrase whose meaning is closest to the word in capital letters.

1. OBSCURE
   A. blanched
   B. trivial
   C. recondite
   D. ostracized
   E. uncanny

2. VIRTUE
   A. righteousness
   B. mayhem
   C. chaos
   D. bedlam
   E. pandemonium

3. FURTIVELY
   A. virtuously
   B. ravenously
   C. voraciously
   D. covertly
   E. rapaciously

4. RAVENOUS
   A. remote
   B. famished
   C. chafing
   D. moot
   E. sadistic

Analogies: Select the answer choice that best completes the meaning of the sentence.

5. Aversion is to animosity as
   A. obscure is to microscopic
   B. chafing is to relaxed
   C. disinclination is to antipathy
   D. prehistoric is to new
   E. remote is to near

6. Evil is to rectitude as
   A. prominence is to fame
   B. chaos is to order
   C. impasse is to dead end
   D. capriciousness is to fickleness
   E. sadism is to cruelty

Sentence Completions: Choose the word that, when inserted in the sentence, <u>best</u> fits the meaning of the sentence as a whole.

7. Walking _____ past the basilisk, Diego made sure to remain unseen and unheard.
   A. obscurely
   B. prehistorically
   C. virtuously
   D. ravenously
   E. stealthily

8. Felicia had a(n) _____ to caraway seeds and carefully avoided all recipes that used them.
   A. contingency
   B. eventuality
   C. tribute
   D. aversion
   E. impasse

1. **C.** *Obscure* and *recondite* both mean *unclear* or *difficult to understand.* Let's see if you remember the rest of the choices. *Blanched* means *turned white, trivial* means *unimportant, ostracized* means *excluded,* and *uncanny* means *remarkable.*

2. **A.** *Virtue* and *righteousness* mean *goodness. Mayhem, chaos, bedlam,* and *pandemonium* mean *disorder.*

3. **D.** *Furtively* and *covertly* both mean *secretly. Covertly* is an easy word to remember—it even looks like *covered—secret. Ravenously, voraciously,* and *rapaciously* mean *very hungry.*

4. **B.** *Ravenous* and *famished* both mean *very hungry.* Remember to use the process of elimination—cross off answers that **definitely** don't work and choose the best of what's left. *Remote* means *far away, chafing* means *irritating, moot* means *irrelevant* or *uncertain,* and *sadistic* means *cruel.*

5. **C.** "Aversion is a synonym of animosity."
   A. Obscure (unclear) is a synonym of microscopic (tiny) . . . no way, don't over think it—*tiny* things may look *unclear,* but these words are definitely not synonyms.
   B. Chafing (irritating) is a synonym of relaxed . . . no.
   C. Disinclination is a synonym of antipathy . . . yes, they both mean *aversion.*
   D. Prehistoric is a synonym of new . . . no, they are opposites.
   E. Remote is a synonym of near . . . no, they are opposites.

6. **B.** "Evil is the opposite of rectitude (goodness)."
   A. Prominence is the opposite of fame . . . no, they have similar meanings.
   B. Chaos (disorder) is the opposite of order . . . yes!
   C. Impasse is the opposite of dead end . . . no, they are synonyms.
   D. Capriciousness is the opposite of fickleness . . . no, they are synonyms.
   E. Sadism is the opposite of cruelty . . . no, they are synonyms.

7. **E.** "Walking <u>*unseen and unheard*</u> past the basilisk, Diego made sure to remain unseen and unheard."
   Stealthily means *secretly* and fits best. Watch out for choice A, *obscurely,* which means *unclearly.* If Diego is unseen, you could say that he is unclear, but that's a stretch, and choice E, *stealthily,* fits the flow of the sentence way better.

8. **D.** "Felicia had a(n) <u>*avoidance*</u> to caraway seeds and carefully avoided all recipes that used them."
   Aversion means *avoidance.*

Quiz 1

I. Let's review some of the words that you've seen in Groups 1–5. Match each of the following words to the correct definition or synonym on the right. Then check the solutions on page 171.

1. Callous	A. Endless
2. Relentless	B. Impending
3. Prophetic	C. Sullen
4. Imminent	D. Remarkable
5. Impasse	E. Insensitive
6. Morose	F. Prescient
7. Uncanny	G. Far away
8. Reciprocate	H. Stalemate
9. Fickle	I. Capricious
10. Remote	J. Requite
11. Trio	K. Recovery
12. Convalescence	L. Insatiable
13. Obscure	M. Rectitude
14. Virtue	N. Abstruse
15. Ravenous	O. Group of three

II. Let's review several of the word parts that you've seen in Groups 1–5. Match each of the following word parts to the correct definition or synonym on the right. Then check the solutions on page 171.

16. -less	A. Not
17. Extra-	B. Without
18. Pre-	C. Again
19. Im-	D. Beyond
20. Micro-	E. Before
21. Re-	F. Very small

Thwarted Plans

Find each of the following words on the *New Moon* page number provided. Based on the way each word is used in the book, guess at its definition.

1. **Authoritative** (p. 30) might mean _____

   _____

2. **Masochistic** (p. 32) might mean _____

   _____

3. **Absolutely** (p. 33) might mean _____

   _____

4. **Devoid** (p. 36) might mean _____

   _____

5. **Deity** (p. 37) might mean _____

   _____

6. **Thwarted** (p. 37) might mean _____

   _____

7. **Brevity** (p. 38) might mean _____

   _____

8. **Indecipherable** (p. 42) might mean _____

   _____

Let's see how you did. Check your answers, write the exact definitions, and reread the sentence in *New Moon* where each word appears. Then complete the drills on the next page.

1. **Authoritative** (p. 30) means *with authority* or *commanding*—you've gotta love Carlisle. While we are on this word, I have to mention the great SAT word, *imperious,* that stumps most students. *Imperious,* like *authoritative,* means *commanding,* but *imperious* also means *bossy.* Recognize the word *imperious?* Think Harry Potter. The Imperius Curse, one of the three Unforgivable Curses, gives the user **control** over another person. J. K. Rowling, like Stephenie Meyer, is looking out for your test scores!

2. **Masochistic** (p. 32) means *enjoying or seeking pain.* It is sort of the opposite of *sadistic* from Group 1, which means *enjoying others' pain.*

3. **Absolutely** (p. 33) means *completely.* Great synonyms of *absolute:* unconditional, unmitigated, unqualified, untempered. If you used *Defining Twilight,* you probably recognize these words. *Conditional, mitigated, qualified,* and *tempered* all mean *not complete.* These words come up a bunch on tests. The SAT, ACT, GED, and SSAT favor reading passages with mild, inoffensive tones, so the answer to an attitude question often uses one of these words to express moderate, inoffensive feelings, such as *qualified admiration* (partial respect), *conditional acceptance* (partial acceptance), or *tempered dislike* (partial dislike).

4. **Devoid** (p. 36) means *empty. Devoid* contains the word *void,* which also means *empty.*

5. **Deity** (p. 37) means *god or goddess.*

6. **Thwarted** (p. 37) means *prevented.* Synonyms: foiled, stymied.

7. **Brevity** (p. 38) means *shortness. Brevity* comes from the word *brief.* In *Hamlet,* Shakespeare says, "Brevity is the soul of wit." He means if you want to be witty, keep it short.

8. **Indecipherable** (p. 42) means *not readable* or *not understandable.* That makes sense, since *in-* means *not,* and *decipher* means *figure out.* Synonym: inscrutable.

Synonyms: Select the word or phrase whose meaning is closest to the word in capital letters.

24

Drills

1. DEVOID
   A. authoritative
   B. imperious
   C. masochistic
   D. empty
   E. brief

2. THWARTED
   A. prevented
   B. qualified
   C. mitigated
   D. tempered
   E. gluttonous

3. INDECIPHERABLE
   A. chafing
   B. unreadable
   C. prehistoric
   D. virtuous
   E. averse

4. ABSOLUTE
   A. total
   B. furtive
   C. covert
   D. clandestine
   E. surreptitious

Analogies: Select the answer choice that best completes the meaning of the sentence.

5. Absolute is to conditional as
   A. indecipherable is to inscrutable
   B. deity is to goddess
   C. brevity is to lengthiness
   D. vampire is to werewolf
   E. thwart is to prevent

6. Authoritative is to commanding as
   A. masochistic is to moot
   B. imperious is to bossy
   C. ceasing is to beginning
   D. remote is to near
   E. uncanny is to ordinary

Sentence Completions: Choose the word or words that, when inserted in the sentence, best fits the meaning of the sentence as a whole.

7. More _____ than any previous teacher, Mr. Capazzi conducted the study hall with _____ discipline, intolerant of disobedience or disorder of any kind.
   A. devoid .. complete
   B. authoritative .. absolute
   C. imperious .. thwarted
   D. masochistic .. total
   E. indecipherable .. brief

8. Jamal believed that the song was not _____ of meaning, but actually full of hidden messages.
   A. ravenous
   B. voracious
   C. insatiable
   D. rapacious
   E. devoid

1. **D.** *Devoid* means *empty. Authoritative* means *commanding—with authority. Imperious* means *bossy,* and *masochistic* means *liking pain.*

2. **A.** *Thwarted* means *prevented. Qualified, mitigated,* and *tempered* mean *not complete. Gluttonous* means *very hungry* or *greedy,* and oddly, it also means *like a wolverine.*

3. **B.** *Indecipherable* means *not decipherable* or *unreadable. Chafing* means *irritating, prehistoric* means *very old, virtuous* means *good,* and *averse* means *opposed.*

4. **A.** *Absolute* means *complete* or *total. Furtive, covert, clandestine,* and *surreptitious* mean *secretive.*

5. **C.** "Absolute (complete) is the opposite of conditional (not complete)."
   - A. Indecipherable is the opposite of inscrutable . . . no, they both mean *not understandable.*
   - B. Deity is the opposite of goddess . . . no, a goddess is a deity.
   - (C.) Brevity (briefness) is the opposite of lengthiness . . . yes!
   - D. Vampire is the opposite of werewolf . . . not really, but don't tell that to Jacob.
   - E. Thwart is the opposite of prevent . . . no, they are synonyms.

6. **B.** "Authoritative means commanding."
   - A. Masochistic (liking pain) means moot (uncertain) . . . no.
   - (B.) Imperious means bossy . . . yes.
   - C. Ceasing means beginning . . . no, they are opposites.
   - D. Remote means near . . . no, they are opposites.
   - E. Uncanny means ordinary . . . no, they are opposites.

7. **B.** "More *into discipline* than any previous teacher, Mr. Capazzi conducted the study hall with *strict* discipline, intolerant of disobedience or disorder of any kind."

   Think of a word that you'd like to see for each blank, pulling a word right from the sentence when possible. Use the process of elimination, one blank at a time. It's often easier to start with the second blank, since by then you have more of the sentence to work with. *Authoritative* means *commanding,* and *absolute* means *total.*

8. **E.** "Jamal believed that the song was not *????* of meaning, but actually full of hidden messages."

   The "but" in this sentence tells you that the word for the blank will be the opposite of "full of." This is a great SAT sentence-completion strategy: words like "but," "although," and "however" indicate that the second part of the sentence opposes the first. *Devoid* means *empty. Ravenous, voracious, insatiable,* and *rapacious* mean *very hungry.*

Group 7

Macabre

Find each of the following words on the *New Moon* page number provided. Based on the way each word is used in the book, guess at its definition.

1. **Macabre** (p. 42) might mean _____

   _____

2. **Impassive** (p. 43) might mean _____

   _____

3. **Serpentine** (p. 44) might mean _____

   _____

4. **Melodramatic** (p. 45) might mean _____

   _____

5. **Wallow** (p. 45) might mean _____

   _____

6. **Remorse** (p. 45) might mean _____

   _____

7. **Piqued** (p. 51) might mean _____

   _____

8. **Elusive** (p. 51) might mean _____

   _____

Let's see how you did. Check your answers, write the exact definitions, and reread the sentence in *New Moon* where each word appears. Then complete the drills on the next page.

1. **Macabre** (p. 42) means *bloody, deathly,* or *gruesome.* Synonyms: ghastly, gory, morbid.

2. **Impassive** (p. 43) means *not feeling or showing emotion.* This is a cool word to break apart. *Im-* means *not,* as in *impatient* (not patient), and *passive* means *allowing.* So *impassive* means ___**not allowing**___ others to see one's feelings. Synonyms: inscrutable, stoic. *Inscrutable* was also a synonym for *indecipherable* in Group 6. It makes sense that *impassive* and *indecipherable* would share a synonym, since *impassive* implies that a person's feelings are hard to decipher.

3. **Serpentine** (p. 44) means *winding,* like the movements of a serpent (snake).

4. **Melodramatic** (p. 45) means *very dramatic.* Synonyms: histrionic, operatic.

5. **Wallow** (p. 45) means *immerse oneself.* This word actually comes from a pig *wallowing* in mud.

6. **Remorse** (p. 45) means *regret.* Synonyms: compunction, contrition, penitence, repentance, ruefulness.

7. **Piqued** (p. 51) in this case means *irritated* or *hurt.* That's easy to remember since *piqued* sounds so much like *picked* or even *pricked,* like pricking and *hurting* your finger on a thorn. Synonyms: affronted, slighted. *Piqued* can also mean *stimulated,* as in "The *New Moon* trailer *piqued* my desire to see the movie." This is a perfect example of a word with several meanings that the SAT, ACT, GED, or SSAT might use in a reading comprehension question.

8. **Elusive** (p. 51) means *hard to find or hold on to.* To help you remember this word, let's turn to Will Farrell and *Anchorman*'s Ron Burgundy, who said, "Mm! She's an **elusive** goddess, Mother Nature . . . for she turns away all suitors." (DreamWorks, *Wake Up, Ron Burgundy: The Lost Movie,* 2004) She's **elusive** (hard to hold on to), because she "turns away all *suitors* (wooers, admirers)." Thanks, Ron! Synonyms: equivocal (unclear), evasive, indefinable.

Synonyms: Select the word or phrase whose meaning is closest to the word in capital letters.

1. MACABRE
   A. impassive
   B. inscrutable
   C. operatic
   D. elusive
   E. morbid

2. SERPENTINE
   A. winding
   B. evasive
   C. indefinable
   D. equivocal
   E. imperious

3. MELODRAMATIC
   A. absolute
   B. devoid
   C. histrionic
   D. thwarted
   E. masochistic

4. PIQUED
   A. wallowing
   B. irritated
   C. remote
   D. relenting
   E. mercurial

Analogies: Select the answer choice that best completes the meaning of the sentence.

5. Piqued is to insult as
   A. irritated is to remorse
   B. chafed is to itchy clothing
   C. thwarted is to brevity
   D. aped is to impasse
   E. ostracized is to contingency

6. Remorse is to compunction as
   A. contriteness is to gory
   B. contrition is to impassive
   C. penitence is to regret
   D. repentance is to elusive
   E. ruefulness is to equivocal

Sentence Completions: Choose the word that, when inserted in the sentence, best fits the meaning of the sentence as a whole.

7. Though Drew's face was impassive, his friends knew that he was _____ by Dustan's harsh comments.
   A. affronted
   B. operatic
   C. tempered
   D. obscured
   E. reciprocated

8. Rowan and Sandy loved to build their model train tracks in complex _____ figure eights.
   A. evasive
   B. histrionic
   C. melodramatic
   D. serpentine
   E. ghastly

1. **E.** *Macabre* and *morbid* mean *gruesome,* like the horror movies that Bella seeks out later in *New Moon*. *Impassive* means *inexpressive, inscrutable* means *indecipherable, operatic* means *dramatic (like an opera),* and *elusive* means *hard to find.*

2. **A.** *Serpentine* means *winding,* like the path of a snake. *Evasive, indefinable,* and *equivocal* mean *elusive. Imperious* means *bossy.*

3. **C.** *Melodramatic* and *histrionic* mean *very dramatic. Absolute* means *complete, devoid* means *empty, thwarted* means *prevented,* and *masochistic* means *liking pain.*

4. **B.** *Piqued* means *irritated. Wallowing* means *immersing oneself, remote* means *far away, relenting* means *ending,* and *mercurial* means *unpredictable.*

5. **B.** "A person might be piqued (irritated) by an insult."

   A. A person might be irritated by remorse (regret) . . . maybe.
   B. A person might be chafed (irritated) by itchy clothing . . . yes!
   C. A person might be thwarted (prevented) by brevity (briefness) . . . no.
   D. A person might be aped (imitated) by an impasse (dead end) . . . no.
   E. A person might be ostracized (excluded) by a contingency (possibility) . . . no.

   Choice A seems possible, but then choice B is much clearer, with a more direct relationship. Remember, don't just choose the first answer choice that seems decent; try all the choices.

6. **C.** "Remorse (regret) is a synonym of compunction (regret)."

   A. Contriteness (regret) is a synonym of gory (bloody) . . . no.
   B. Contrition (regret) is a synonym of impassive (unexpressive) . . . no.
   C. Penitence (regret) is a synonym of regret . . . yes!
   D. Repentance (regret) is a synonym of elusive (hard to find) . . . no.
   E. Ruefulness (regret) is a synonym of equivocal (unclear) . . . no.

7. **A.** "Though Drew's face was impassive, his friends knew that he was *harshed/hurt* by Dustan's harsh comments."

   You know the word *impassive* (unemotional), but even if you didn't, you could still get this question correct. The SAT often throws in a tough word that you don't need. So if you see a word in the sentence that you don't know, try crossing it out and doing the question without it. You'll be surprised how well this works! Choice A, *affronted,* means *offended* and is the best answer.

8. **D.** "Rowan and Sandy loved to build their model train tracks in complex *complex/figure eight* figure eights."

   Use the process of elimination. The sentence does not indicate that the tracks are *evasive* (hard to find), *histrionic* (dramatic), *melodramatic,* or *ghastly*. They are *serpentine* (winding).

Group 8
Tenuous Composure

Find each of the following words on the *New Moon* page number provided. Based on the way each word is used in the book, guess at its definition.

1. **Premonition** (p. 52) might mean _____

   _____

2. **Tenuous** (p. 54) might mean _____

   _____

3. **Aloof** (p. 54) might mean _____

   _____

4. **Solicitously** (p. 55) might mean _____

   _____

5. **Indifferently** (p. 56) might mean _____

   _____

6. **Loped** (p. 56) might mean _____

   _____

7. **Interminable** (p. 57) might mean _____

   _____

8. **Composure** (p. 57) might mean _____

   _____

Let's see how you did. Check your answers, write the exact definitions, and reread the sentence in *New Moon* where each word appears. Then complete the drills on the next page.

1. **Premonition** (p. 52) means *feeling that something bad will happen.* *Pre-* means *before* and *monition* means *warning,* so a *premonition* is a **warning before** something happens. Synonyms: foreboding, intuition, presentiment.

2. **Tenuous** (p. 54) means *flimsy* or *unsubstantiated.*

3. **Aloof** (p. 54) means *distant.* This is similar to *remote* from Group 4. *Aloof* and *remote* can both refer to a person being distant, as in cold and uninterested, but *remote* can also mean literally *far away.*

4. **Solicitously** (p. 55) means *with concern or interest.* This is a great high-level SAT and ACT vocabulary word that stumped tons of students on a recent SAT. But it won't stump you, thanks to Stephenie Meyer! To remember this word, think of the signs you've seen on doorways that say "No Solicitors." Solicitors are door-to-door salespeople. When you open the door, they say "So, how are you today?" They express *concern and interest.* That's how the words are connected!

5. **Indifferently** (p. 56) is the opposite of *solicitously.* It means *without concern or interest.* *In-* means *not,* so *indifferent* means *not showing a difference—not caring.* Synonyms: apathetic, dispassionate, nonchalant.

6. **Loped** (p. 56) means *ran or jogged with a graceful stride.* This word has a very specific meaning in horseback riding, where *lope* is a slower variation of *canter* used in western riding.

7. **Interminable** (p. 57) means *endless.* *In-* means *not* and *terminable* means *ending,* so *interminable* means *unending—endless.* Synonyms: ceaseless, incessant.

8. **Composure** (p. 57) means *calmness.* Synonyms: aplomb (calm self-confidence), equanimity, poise, sangfroid (excessive composure under danger), serenity, tranquility. I love the words *aplomb* and *sangfroid*—use those in your SAT, ACT, GED, or SSAT essay, and I guarantee you'll gain points!

Synonyms: Select the word or phrase whose meaning is closest to the word in capital letters.

1. PREMONITION
   A. composure
   B. aversion
   C. foreboding
   D. convalescence
   E. mayhem

2. SOLICITOUS
   A. concerned
   B. tenuous
   C. composed
   D. nonchalant
   E. dispassionate

3. INDIFFERENT
   A. inexorable
   B. extraordinary
   C. wizened
   D. prophetic
   E. apathetic

4. INTERMINABLE
   A. macabre
   B. incessant
   C. impassive
   D. melodramatic
   E. elusive

Analogies: Select the answer choice that best completes the meaning of the sentence.

5. Composure is to aplomb as
   A. serenity is to indifference
   B. equanimity is to contingency
   C. poise is to reverie
   D. serenity is to sangfroid
   E. tranquility is to enmity

6. Loped is to walked as
   A. wallowed is to piqued
   B. basilisk is to thwarted
   C. ran is to jogged
   D. chaffed is to blanched
   E. wizened is to tolled

Sentence Completions: Choose the word or words that, when inserted in the sentence, best fits the meaning of the sentence as a whole.

7. Initially, Lucas mistook Emily's _____ manner for _____ and even-temperedness, rather than disinterest.
   A. aloof .. interminable
   B. indifferent .. equanimity
   C. solicitous .. sangfroid
   D. tenuous .. callous
   E. distant .. serpentine

8. The election results confirmed the validity of Mae-Li's _____ that her party would lose by a landslide.
   A. composure
   B. remorse
   C. compunction
   D. foreboding
   E. contrition

1. **C.** *Premonition* and *foreboding* mean *predicting. Composure* means *calm, aversion* means *avoidance, convalescence* means *recovery,* and *mayhem* means *disorder.*

2. **A.** *Solicitous* means *concerned. Tenuous* means *flimsy, composed* means *calm,* and *nonchalant* and *dispassionate* mean *without interest.*

3. **E.** *Indifferent* and *apathetic* mean *without interest. Inexorable* means *unstoppable, extraordinary* means *beyond ordinary, wizened* means *wrinkled,* and *prophetic* means *predicting.*

4. **B.** *Interminable* and *incessant* both mean *not ending. Macabre* means *gruesome, impassive* means *not showing feeling, melodramatic* means *very dramatic,* and *elusive* means *hard to find.*

5. **D.** "Composure (calmness) is a synonym for aplomb (calm confidence)."
   - A. Serenity (calmness) is a synonym for indifference (disinterest) . . . maybe, but it's a stretch.
   - B. Equanimity (calmness) is a synonym for contingency (possibility) . . . no.
   - C. Poise (calmness) is a synonym for reverie (thoughts) . . . no.
   - (D.) Serenity (calmness) is a synonym for sangfroid (calmness) . . . yes! *Sangfroid* is a cool word to break apart. In French, *sang* means *blood,* and *froid* means *cold.* So *sangfroid* means *"cold blood"*—staying cool under pressure, calm and collected.
   - E. Tranquility (calmness) is a synonym for enmity (hatred) . . . no.

6. **C.** "Loped (jogged) is faster than walked."
   - A. Wallowed (immersed in) is faster than piqued (irritated) . . . no.
   - B. Basilisk (legendary creature) is faster than thwarted (prevented) . . . no.
   - (C.) Ran is faster than jogged . . . yes!
   - D. Chaffed (irritated) is faster than blanched (turned white) . . . no.
   - E. Wizened (wrinkled) is faster than tolled (rang) . . . no.

7. **B.** "Initially, Lucas mistook Emily's *disinterested* manner for *even-temperedness* and even-temperedness, rather than disinterest."
   Indifferent means *disinterested,* and *equanimity* means *even-temperedness.*

8. **D.** "The election results confirmed the validity of Mae-Li's *fear/intuition* that her party would lose by a landslide."
   Foreboding means *prediction that something bad will happen* (*fore-* means *before,* and *-bode* means *predict—predict before!*). Choices B, C, and E, which all mean *remorse,* might happen from losing by a landslide, but would not "confirm" it. Make sure your choice is supported by evidence in the question.

Group 9
Precipice

Find each of the following words on the *New Moon* page number provided. Based on the way each word is used in the book, guess at its definition.

1. **Heady** (p. 58) might mean _____

   _____

2. **Precipice** (p. 60) might mean _____

   _____

3. **Compulsion** (p. 60) might mean _____

   _____

4. **Meddling** (p. 61) might mean _____

   _____

5. **Sinister** (p. 63) might mean _____

   _____

6. **Tolerant** (p. 65) might mean _____

   _____

7. **Reserved** (p. 65) might mean _____

   _____

8. **Sieve** (p. 72) might mean _____

   _____

Let's see how you did. Check your answers, write the exact definitions, and reread the sentence in *New Moon* where each word appears. Then complete the drills on the next page.

1. **Heady** (p. 58) in this case means *very powerful*. Bella was trying to convince herself that everything would go back to normal, and when she saw Edward's car, she felt *overwhelming* (very powerful) relief. *Heady* can also mean *intoxicating* (making drunk), *thrilling,* or *cerebral* (mental, brainy). Standardized tests often ask you to determine how a word with several meanings was used in a reading passage.

2. **Precipice** (p. 60) means *cliff.* Synonyms: bluff, crag, escarpment, scarp. The SSAT loves to use nature words like these. Some other examples from recent tests are *bough* (tree branch), *aviary* (a place where birds are kept), and *abyss* (chasm—a deep gorge or ravine).

3. **Compulsion** (p. 60) means *obsession. Compulsion* comes from the word *compel,* which means *require.* An **obsession requires** a person to do something, such as think about Edward day and night.

4. **Meddling** (p. 61) means *interfering.* Of course, the most famous and important literary use of this word is when the villain in every *Scooby-Doo* episode says at the end of the show, "And I would have gotten away with it, too, if it wasn't for you **meddling** kids!" (Warner Home Video, *Chill Out, Scooby-Doo!*, 2007)

5. **Sinister** (p. 63) means *wicked.* Synonyms: baleful, depraved, heinous, impious, iniquitous, malevolent, menacing, nefarious, pernicious.

6. **Tolerant** (p. 65) means *patient* or *forgiving.* Synonyms: forbearing, indulgent, lenient.

7. **Reserved** (p. 65) means *holding back or not showing one's feelings.* That makes sense since when you **reserve** a seat for your friend, you are **holding it back** from others taking it. Synonyms: aloof, introverted, reticent, taciturn.

8. **Sieve** (p. 72) literally means a *strainer,* like one you might use to rinse off vegetables. Figuratively it implies that someone forgets easily, with memories running through the strainer like water. I know that it's hard to discuss such mundane issues like vocabulary right now, when we're in such a heart-wrenching part of the book, but don't worry, we're in it together.

Synonyms: Select the word or phrase whose meaning is closest to the word in capital letters.

1. PRECIPICE
   A. heady
   B. intoxicating
   C. crag
   D. cerebral
   E. compulsion

2. MEDDLING
   A. sinister
   B. interfering
   C. baleful
   D. depraved
   E. heinous

3. TOLERANT
   A. bluff
   B. escarpment
   C. scarp
   D. lenient
   E. solicitous

4. RESERVED
   A. reticent
   B. indulgent
   C. forbearing
   D. impious
   E. iniquitous

Analogies: Select the answer choice that best completes the meaning of the sentence.

5. Indifferent is to meddle as
   A. sinister is to tolerate
   B. reserved is to hold back
   C. obsessed is to give up
   D. aloof is to thwart
   E. loping is to run

6. Compulsion is to obsession as
   A. precipice is to aviary
   B. bough is to chasm
   C. void is to deity
   D. sieve is to strainer
   E. basilisk is to vampire

Sentence Completions: Choose the word or words that, when inserted in the sentence, <u>best</u> fits the meaning of the sentence as a whole.

7. Unable to stop herself, Leigh felt _____ to approach the _____ and look over the ledge to the five-hundred-foot drop below.
   A. tolerant .. chasm
   B. compelled .. precipice
   C. forced .. bough
   D. reserved .. premonition
   E. urged .. aviary

8. Zach argued that Carnage was thoroughly menacing, the most _____ villain ever to battle Spiderman.
   A. meddling
   B. forbearing
   C. indulgent
   D. solicitous
   E. sinister

1. **C.** *Precipice* and *crag* mean *cliff.* *Heady* means *powerful, intoxication*
   means *drunkenness, cerebral* means *mental,* and *compulsion* means
   obsession. Interestingly, the word *intoxication* breaks down to *in-*
   meaning *in,* and *toxic,* which means *poison.* So, *intoxication* means
   taking in poison. Drinking and "drugs are bad, mmmkay." (Mr.
   Mackey, *South Park,* Comedy Central, 1998)
2. **B.** *Meddling* means *interfering. Sinister, baleful, depraved,* and *heinous*
   mean *wicked.*
3. **D.** *Tolerant* means *lenient.* More great nature words: *bluff,*
   escarpment, and *scarp* mean *cliff. Solicitous* means *interested* or
   concerned.
4. **A.** *Reserved* and *reticent* both mean *not showing one's feelings—*
   holding back. Indulgent and *forbearing* mean *tolerant. Impious* and
   iniquitous mean *wicked.*
5. **C.** "An indifferent person does not meddle."
   A. A sinister (wicked) person does not tolerate (allow) . . .
      maybe, but that's probably too much of a stretch. Let's
      check out the other choices before we eliminate it.
   B. A reserved (held back) person does not hold back . . . no,
      they do.
   C. An obsessed person does not give up . . . yes, that's a much
      clearer answer than choice A.
   D. An aloof (held back) person does not thwart (prevent) . . . no,
      that makes no sense.
   E. A loping (gracefully running) person does not run . . . no,
      they do.
6. **D.** "A compulsion is an obsession."
   A. A precipice (cliff) is an aviary (place to keep birds) . . . not
      really.
   B. A bough (tree branch) is a chasm (deep ravine) . . . no.
   C. A void (empty) is a deity (god or goddess) . . . no.
   D. A sieve is a strainer . . . yes!
   E. A basilisk is a vampire . . . no way, and everyone knows that
      basilisks don't really exist!
7. **B.** "Unable to stop herself, Leigh felt <u>urged</u> to approach the <u>ledge</u>
   and look over the ledge to the five-hundred-foot drop below."
      Use the process of elimination, one blank at a time. You
   can eliminate choices A and D for the first blank, and you can
   eliminate choices C, D, and E for the second blank. That leaves
   only choice B! *Compelled* means *urged* or *forced. Precipice* means *cliff.*
8. **E.** "Zach argued that Carnage was thoroughly menacing, the
   most <u>menacing</u> villain ever to battle Spiderman."
      Sinister means *wicked* and is the best choice.

Group 10
Severed!

Find each of the following words on the *New Moon* page number provided. Based on the way each word is used in the book, guess at its definition.

1. **Tranquil** (p. 72) might mean _____

_____

2. **Severed** (p. 72) might mean _____

_____

3. **Supple** (p. 76) might mean _____

_____

4. **Prodded** (p. 78) might mean _____

_____

5. **Surreptitiously** (p. 78) might mean _____

_____

6. **Inevitable** (p. 82) might mean _____

_____

7. **Lurched** (p. 83) might mean _____

_____

8. **Exasperation** (p. 94) might mean _____

_____

Let's see how you did. Check your answers, write the exact definitions,
and reread the sentence in *New Moon* where each word appears. Then
complete the drills on the next page.

1. **Tranquil** (p. 72) means *calm.* Synonyms: pacific, placid, serene.
   Water is often described as calming, such as the Pacific Ocean
   and Lake Placid in New York State, home of the 1980 Winter
   Olympics.

2. **Severed** (p. 72) means *broken* or *cut apart.* If you google "severed,"
   you get several entries for *Severed,* a 2005 zombie horror film with
   the line, "You have to **sever** the head; it's the only way to kill
   them." (Forest of the Dead Productions) Gross, but now you'll
   never forget this word, and you're prepared for Bella's horror
   movies.

3. **Supple** (p. 76) means *graceful* and *flexible.* I love the scene in
   Superbad, when Evan says, "It's not just making them smaller.
   They completely reshaped them. They made them more supple,
   symmetrical," to which Seth responds, "I gotta catch a glimpse of
   those warlocks. Let's make a move." (Columbia Pictures, 2007)
   Synonyms: limber, lissome, lithe, nimble, willowy.

4. **Prodded** (p. 78) means *urged.* It comes from the word *prod* (to
   poke) as in *prodding* cattle to move forward. Synonyms for *prod:*
   cajole, coax, enjoin, entreat, exhort, goad, implore, incite, spur.

5. **Surreptitiously** (p. 78) was a synonym for *furtively* in Group 5 and
   means *secretly.* The other synonyms were *clandestinely, covertly,* and
   stealthily.

6. **Inevitable** (p. 82) means *unavoidable.* "Inevitable" has been in the
   title of songs by Shakira, Squirrel Nut Zippers, Koopsta Knicca,
   DJ Keoki, Halifax, Anberlin, and Mushroomhead. We've pretty
   much got the spectrum of musical tastes covered. *Inevitable* means
   the same thing as *inexorable* from Group 1.

7. **Lurched** (p. 83) means *jerked* or *staggered.*

8. **Exasperation** (p. 94) means *irritation.* This is an interesting word
   to break apart. *Ex-* means *out,* and *asperat* refers to *blowing air.* So
   exasperation means *blowing air out,* which is what lots of people do
   when they are irritated; they huff and sigh and humph.

Synonyms: Select the word or phrase whose meaning is closest to the word in capital letters.

1. TRANQUIL
   A. severed
   B. limber
   C. pacific
   D. lissome
   E. willowy

2. SUPPLE
   A. lithe
   B. furtive
   C. clandestine
   D. covert
   E. exasperated

3. PROD
   A. meddle
   B. implore
   C. tolerate
   D. pique
   E. relent

4. SURREPTITIOUS
   A. covert
   B. authoritative
   C. absolute
   D. obscure
   E. repentant

Analogies: Select the answer choice that best completes the meaning of the sentence.

5. Inevitable is to inexorable as
   A. prod is to goad
   B. tenuous is to certain
   C. apathetic is to solicitous
   D. interminable is to finished
   E. iniquitous is to angelic

6. Prod is to compel as
   A. quantify is to wizen
   B. mimic is to ape
   C. ostracize is to reciprocate
   D. coax is to require
   E. wallow is to chafe

Sentence Completions: Choose the word that, when inserted in the sentence, <u>best</u> fits the meaning of the sentence as a whole.

7. Boone was shocked that his sister, Shannon, could appear so _____ as their plane lurched with each new pocket of turbulence that it hit.
   A. severed
   B. supple
   C. surreptitious
   D. serene
   E. exasperated

8. A dancer must be _____; he or she must be both graceful and flexible.
   A. tranquil
   B. covert
   C. clandestine
   D. stealthy
   E. supple

1. **C.** *Tranquil* and *pacific* mean *peaceful.* If the correct answer does not jump out, use the process of elimination. *Severed* means *cut. Limber, lissome,* and *willowy* mean *flexible.*

2. **A.** *Supple* means *lithe. Furtive, clandestine,* and *covert* mean *secret. Exasperated* means *irritated.*

3. **B.** *Prod* means *urge.* That's also what *implore* means. *Meddle* means *interfere, tolerate* means *allow, pique* means *stimulate,* and *relent* means *give up.*

4. **A.** *Surreptitious* and *covert* mean *secret. Authoritative* means *commanding, absolute* means *complete, obscure* means *unclear,* and *repentant* means *regretful.*

5. **A.** "Inevitable means the same thing as inexorable."
   - **A.** Prod means the same thing as goad . . . yes, they both mean *urge.*
   - B . Tenuous (uncertain) means the same thing as certain . . . no.
   - C . Apathetic (disinterested) means the same thing as solicitous (interested) . . . no.
   - D . Interminable (endless) means the same thing as finished . . . no, they are opposites.
   - E . Iniquitous (wicked) means the same thing as angelic . . . no.

6. **D.** "Prod (urge) is less strong than compel (require)."
   - A . Quantify (count) is less strong than wizen (wrinkle) . . . no.
   - B . Mimic (imitate) is less strong than ape . . . no, they mean the same thing.
   - C . Ostracize (exclude) is less strong than reciprocate (give back) . . . no.
   - **D.** Coax (urge) is less strong than require . . . yes!
   - E . Wallow (immerse in) is less strong than chafe (irritate) . . . no.

   Don't convince yourself that *immerse in* is less extreme than *irritate.* If you can't make the link in one sentence, then it's not the correct answer.

7. **D.** "Boone was shocked that his sister, Shannon, could appear so <u>????</u> as their plane lurched with each new pocket of turbulence that it hit."

   If you can't think of a word to fill the blank, try the choices and use the process of elimination. Since turbulence is stressful, Boone probably would not be shocked if Shannon was *exasperated* (irritated). The choices *severed* (cut in two), *supple* (flexible), and *surreptitious* (secretive) also don't make sense. Boone would be shocked if she remained totally calm, so choice D (serene) is best.

8. **E.** "A dancer must be <u>graceful and flexible;</u> he or she must be both graceful and flexible."

   Use evidence from the sentence—you want a word for *graceful and flexible. Tranquil* and *stealthy* sound decent in the first part of the sentence, but don't fit with *graceful and flexible.* Choice E, *supple,* means *graceful and flexible* and fits best.

Quiz 2

I. Let's review some of the words that you've seen in Groups 6–10. Match each of the following words to the correct definition or synonym on the right. Then check the solutions on page 171.

1. Absolute	A. Empty
2. Devoid	B. Gruesome
3. Brevity	C. Irritated
4. Macabre	D. Concerned
5. Impassive	E. Complete
6. Piqued	F. Shortness
7. Tenuous	G. Unemotional
8. Solicitous	H. Endless
9. Interminable	I. Placid
10. Precipice	J. Goad
11. Meddling	K. Flimsy
12. Sinister	L. Crag
13. Tranquil	M. Lithe
14. Supple	N. Interfering
15. Prod	O. Baleful

II. Let's review several of the word parts that you've seen in Groups 6–10. Match each of the following word parts to the correct definition or synonym on the right. Then check the solutions on page 171.

16. Pre-	A. Poison
17. In-, Im-	B. Before
18. Ex-	C. Not
19. Toxic	D. Out
20. Fore-	E. Predict
21. -Bode	F. Before

Morose

Find each of the following words on the *New Moon* page number provided. Based on the way each word is used in the book, guess at its definition.

1. **Mystification** (p. 95) might mean _____

   _____

2. **Moroseness** (p. 95) might mean _____

   _____

3. **Grimace** (p. 96) might mean _____

   _____

4. **Monotone** (p. 98) might mean _____

   _____

5. **Communism** (p. 99) might mean _____

   _____

6. **Curriculum** (p. 99) might mean _____

   _____

7. **Antisocial** (p. 99) might mean _____

   _____

8. **Loitered** (p. 100) might mean _____

   _____

Let's see how you did. Check your answers, write the exact definitions, and reread the sentence in *New Moon* where each word appears. Then complete the drills on the next page.

1. **Mystification** (p. 95) means *confusion*. That's easy to remember since *mystification* is so similar to the word *mystery*.

2. **Moroseness** (p. 95) means *gloominess*. Bella says she was ". . . careful to avoid all forms of moroseness, moping included," so moroseness must be related to moping—that's enough to get the gist of the word and a test question correct! Synonyms for *morose:* doleful, dour, glum, lugubrious, melancholic, sullen.

3. **Grimace** (p. 96) means *an expression of pain or disgust*. Grimace is, of course, also an odd-shaped purple creature in McDonaldland, but I doubt that the SAT will ask you about that.

4. **Monotone** (p. 98) means *a flat, dull tone*. *Mono-* means *one,* so literally, *monotone* means *one toned*. Try to speak without altering your tone at all, and you'll see that it's pretty **flat and dull.**

5. **Communism** (p. 99) is *a political philosophy in which all property is publicly owned*. Communism has a pretty bad rap in the United States, but at least you can use the root *com-* to raise your test scores. *Com-* means *together.* That helps you remember some tough words, such as *comity* (a group of nations), *commingle* (mix together), *commiserate* (feel sympathy with), and *compendious* (information grouped together in a short but complete way).

6. **Curriculum** (p. 99) means *plan of study*.

7. **Antisocial** (p. 99) means *not social* or *solitary*. *Anti-* means *not* or *against,* so that's why *antisocial* means *not social*.

8. **Loitered** (p. 100) means *hung around*. Earlier, I talked about signs that say "No Soliciting." There are also signs that say "No Loitering." That means, "Don't **hang around** on our stoop and block shoppers from coming in."

Synonyms: Select the word or phrase whose meaning is closest to the word in capital letters.

1. MYSTIFY
   A. grimace
   B. loiter
   C. confuse
   D. enjoin
   E. entreat

2. MOROSE
   A. pacific
   B. dour
   C. inexorable
   D. nimble
   E. limber

3. MONOTONE
   A. solitary
   B. compendious
   C. antisocial
   D. commingled
   E. flat

4. COMITY
   A. group of numbers
   B. group of nations
   C. coven of vampires
   D. pack of wolves
   E. humorous movie

Analogies: Select the answer choice that best completes the meaning of the sentence.

5. Curriculum is to studies as
   A. mimic is to premonitions
   B. tawny is to yellowish-brown
   C. tribute is to homage
   D. ostracism is to inclusion
   E. anarchy is to order

6. Morose is to melancholic as
   A. monotone is to mellow
   B. grimace is to purple
   C. willowy is to furtive
   D. doleful is to dour
   E. heady is to nefarious

Sentence Completions: Choose the word or words that, when inserted in the sentence, <u>best</u> fits the meaning of the sentence as a whole.

7. Shopkeepers in downtown Georgetown were _____ by the excessive _____, which blocked their doorways and prevented patrons from entering.
   A. incited .. lugubriousness
   B. coaxed .. curriculum
   C. exasperated .. loitering
   D. thwarted .. serenity
   E. chaffed .. compulsion

8. Lian sought a _____ volume that was short enough to read in one sitting, yet presented all of the essential facts on the matter.
   A. curricular
   B. lugubrious
   C. mystifying
   D. monotone
   E. compendious

1. **C.** *Mystify* means *confuse. Grimace* means *frown, loiter* means *hang around,* and *enjoin* and *entreat* mean *urge.*

2. **B.** *Morose* and *dour* mean *sad. Pacific* means *calm, inexorable* means *unstoppable,* and *nimble* and *limber* mean *flexible.*

3. **E.** *Monotone* means *one-toned, dull, and* **flat.** If *flat* did not jump right out at you, use the process of elimination. *Solitary* comes from *solo-,* which means *alone. Compendious* contains *com-,* meaning *together,* and means *lots of information grouped concisely* **together.** *Antisocial* means *not social* and *commingled* means *mixed* **together.**

4. **B.** *Comity* also contains *com-* (together) and can mean *a group of nations. Humorous movie* is a nice trick answer since it sounds like *comedy,* but it is not related.

5. **C.** "Curriculum is a plan of study." It's great when you can define the first word using the second. If this was a tough question for you, rely on the process of elimination.
    A. Mimic (imitate) is a plan of premonitions (predictions) . . . no.
    B. Tawny is a plan of yellowish-brown . . . no, *tawny* means *yellowish-brown,* but is not a "plan."
    C. Tribute is a plan of homage . . . yes! A *tribute* can be a plan to pay *homage* (respect).
    D. Ostracism is a plan of inclusion . . . no, *ostracism* means *exclusion.*
    E. Anarchy is a plan of order . . . no, *anarchy* means *disorder.*

6. **D.** "Morose (sad) and melancholic (sad) are synonyms."
    A. Monotone (one-toned, dull) and mellow are synonyms . . . maybe, but it's a stretch.
    B. Grimace and purple are synonyms . . . not unless you live in McDonaldland.
    C. Willowy (flexible) and furtive (secretive) are synonyms . . . no.
    D. Doleful (sad) and dour (sad) are synonyms . . . yes, and a much stronger choice than A.
    E. Heady (powerful or cerebral) and nefarious (wicked) are synonyms . . . no.

7. **C.** "Shopkeepers in downtown Georgetown were _upset_ by the excessive _door blocking,_ which blocked their doorways and prevented patrons from entering."
    Use the process of elimination, one blank at a time. If you can't think of a word to fill a blank, you can look for evidence in the sentence and decide if the word should be positive or negative. Then try the choices, and remember to eliminate only choices that **definitely** do not work. *Exasperated* means *irritated,* and *loitering* means *hanging around.*

8. **E.** "Lian sought a _short but complete_ volume that was short enough to read in one sitting, yet presented all of the essential facts on the matter." *Compendious* means *short but complete.*

A Nebulous Threat

Find each of the following words on the *New Moon* page number provided. Based on the way each word is used in the book, guess at its definition.

1. **Mollified** (p. 101) might mean _____

   _____

2. **Tentative** (p. 102) might mean _____

   _____

3. **Infuse** (p. 103) might mean _____

   _____

4. **Twilight** (p. 105) might mean _____

   _____

5. **Exposition** (p. 105) might mean _____

   _____

6. **Haggard** (p. 106) might mean _____

   _____

7. **Grotesque** (p. 106) might mean _____

   _____

8. **Nebulous** (p. 110) might mean _____

   _____

Let's see how you did. Check your answers, write the exact definitions, and reread the sentence in *New Moon* where each word appears. Then complete the drills on the next page.

Definitions

1. **Mollified** (p. 101) means *soothed*. This word even sounds soothing; my muscles relax as I say it. Sometime when you can't sleep, just say *mollified* twenty times. You'll be asleep by number ten. Synonyms: alleviate, ameliorate, assuage, conciliate, pacify, palliate, placate.

2. **Tentative** (p. 102) means *hesitant*. Let's look at the context. "Jessica smiled at me with **tentative** friendliness. . . . " Here's a great SAT, ACT, GED, or SSAT reading comprehension question: "Why was Jessica hesitant?" Answer: Bella had been an antisocial zombie for four months, so Jessica felt ignored and hurt and was now **hesitant** to open back up to her.

3. **Infuse** (p. 103) means *mix*. This is a terrific word to break apart. *In-* in this case means, well . . . *in;* and *fuse* means *join,* so *infuse* means *join in—mix. Infuse* can also mean *fill* (as in "yoga infuses me with joy"). Next time you visit Starbucks or your local tea shop, practice your vocabulary while you order your decaf chai apple berry soy **infusion** (mixture).

4. **Twilight** (p. 105) refers to *the period after sunset but before darkness.* I love that Stephenie Meyer threw that word in here!

5. **Exposition** (p. 105) means *back-story* or *explanation,* like **exposing** the story of a celebrity's drug use in a shocking **exposé** in *People* magazine, or writing an **expository** essay for English class.

6. **Haggard** (p. 106) means *tired and unhealthy looking,* like a zombie. Can you say Bella?

7. **Grotesque** (p. 106) looks like the word *gross,* and means *very disgusting.*

8. **Nebulous** (p. 110) means *unclear.* The SAT and ACT love this word and its synonyms: ambiguous, amorphous, imprecise, muddled, tenuous, vague.

Synonyms: Select the word or phrase whose meaning is closest to the 49 word in capital letters.

1. MOLLIFIED
   A. exposed
   B. placated
   C. loitered
   D. grimaced
   E. commiserated

2. INFUSE
   A. relent
   B. cease
   C. mix
   D. prophesize
   E. blanch

3. HAGGARD
   A. ambiguous
   B. tired
   C. amorphous
   D. imprecise
   E. muddled

4. NEBULOUS
   A. grotesque
   B. solitary
   C. sullen
   D. morose
   E. muddled

Analogies: Select the answer choice that best completes the meaning of the sentence.

5. Conciliate is to assuage as
   A. mollify is to infuse
   B. pacify is to mix
   C. placate is to expose
   D. alleviate is to thwart
   E. ameliorate is to palliate

6. Tentative is to definite as
   A. ravenous is to voracious
   B. tawny is to colorful
   C. nonchalant is to indifferent
   D. infused is to separate
   E. remorseful is to regretful

Sentence Completions: Choose the word or words that, when inserted in the sentence, best fits the meaning of the sentence as a whole.

7. Jennifer enjoyed watching the light filter through the clouds; twilight _____ her with a sense of peace, _____ her incessant worries.
   A. infused .. pacifying
   B. filled .. irritating
   C. left .. chafing
   D. conveyed .. soothing
   E. exasperated .. appeasing

8. After weeks of nightmares, Bella looked _____ and exhausted.
   A. mystified
   B. antisocial
   C. microscopic
   D. ostracized
   E. haggard

1. **B.** *Mollified* and *placated* mean *soothed. Loitered* means *hung around,* *grimaced* means *frowned, commiserated* means *felt sympathy with.* Interestingly, since com- means *together, commiserated* looks like *miserable together,* which is pretty much what it means.

2. **C.** *Infuse* means *mix. Relent* and *cease* mean *give up* or *end, prophesize* means *predict,* and *blanch* means *turn white.*

3. **B.** *Haggard* means *tired. Ambiguous, amorphous, imprecise,* and *muddled* mean *unclear.*

4. **E.** *Nebulous* and *muddled* both mean *foggy* or *unclear.* You may remember from science class that a nebula is a massive interstellar cloud of dust—*foggy and unclear. Grotesque* means *very disgusting,* and *solitary* means *alone. Sullen* and *morose* mean *sad.*

5. **E.** "Conciliate (soothe) is a synonym for assuage (soothe)."
   A. Mollify (soothe) is a synonym for infuse (mix) . . . no.
   B. Pacify (soothe) is a synonym for mix . . . no.
   C. Placate (soothe) is a synonym for expose . . . no.
   D. Alleviate (soothe) is a synonym for thwart (prevent) . . . no.
   (E.) Ameliorate (soothe) is a synonym for palliate (soothe) . . . yes!

6. **D.** "Tentative (hesitant) is the opposite of definite."
   A. Ravenous is the opposite of voracious . . . no, they both mean *very hungry.*
   B. Tawny is the opposite of colorful . . . no, tawny is a color.
   C. Nonchalant is the opposite of indifferent . . . no, they are synonyms.
   (D.) Infused (mixed) is the opposite of separate . . . yes!
   E. Remorseful is the opposite of regretful . . . no, they are synonyms.

7. **A.** "Jennifer enjoyed watching the light filter through the clouds; twilight _filled_ her with a sense of peace, _easing_ her incessant worries."

   Use the process of elimination, one blank at a time. Choice A is best, since *infused* means *filled* or *mixed,* and *pacifying* means *soothing.* You know that *incessant,* a synonym from Groups 1 and 8, means *constant,* but even if you didn't, you could just ignore it and still get the question correct—that's how sentence completion questions are designed!

8. **E.** "After weeks of nightmares, Bella looked _exhausted_ and exhausted."

   Haggard means *very tired.* Use evidence in the sentence to choose your answer. You know that Bella was in fact *antisocial* and even *ostracized* by many of her friends, and she was *mystified* by the whole situation, but the sentence and the blank are about her being "exhausted."

Group 13
A Beautiful Rebuke

Find each of the following words on the *New Moon* page number provided. Based on the way each word is used in the book, guess at its definition.

1. **Rebuked** (p. 111) might mean _____

   _____

2. **Irate** (p. 111) might mean _____

   _____

3. **Running amuck** (p. 112) might mean _____

   _____

4. **Dithering** (p. 113) might mean _____

   _____

5. **Psychopaths** (p. 115) might mean _____

   _____

6. **Conviction** (p. 116) might mean _____

   _____

7. **Excising** (p. 118) might mean _____

   _____

8. **Sallow** (p. 124) might mean _____

   _____

Let's see how you did. Check your answers, write the exact definitions, and reread the sentence in *New Moon* where each word appears. Then complete the drills on the next page.

1. **Rebuked** (p. 111) means *scolded strongly.* Synonyms: admonished, censured, chastised, reprimanded, reproached, reproved. *Admonished* and *reproached* are *less stern (more gentle) scolds.*

2. **Irate** (p. 111) means *furious.* The context actually defines the word: "It was a **furious** voice, . . . it was **irate.**" Synonyms: incensed, infuriated, livid.

3. **Running amuck** (p. 112) means *being out of control* and comes from the Filipino word *amuk* describing a rampaging elephant.

4. **Dithering** (p. 113) means *being indecisive.* Perhaps that's where the word *ditsy* comes from. A ditsy person would be pretty indecisive. Synonyms: vacillating, wavering.

5. **Psychopaths** (p. 115) are *persons with mental illnesses that lead to violent behavior.* You probably knew this word already, but it's a great word to break apart. *Psycho-* refers to the *mind,* as in *psychology* (study of the mind) and *psychic* (a person with mental powers). And *–path* refers to *disease* or *treatment,* which is why a *psychopath* is *someone with a **mental disease.***

6. **Conviction** (p. 116) means *sureness.* It comes from the word *convince.* When you have *conviction,* you are totally *convinced—you're sure.* Of course, it can also refer to *a jury's pronouncement of guilt.* Synonym: certitude.

7. **Excising** (p. 118) means *removing.* Pretty much any time you see a word that starts with *ex-,* it has to do with something *being removed* or *going away,* like *exception, exit, excursion,* and *ex-boyfriend.* And *cis-* often implies *cut,* as in *scissors.*

8. **Sallow** (p. 124) means *pale.* You have a lot of words for pale. So far in this book you have *blanched* and *sallow,* and if you used *Defining Twilight,* you learned *alabaster, ashen, pallid,* and *wan.* This is a vampire story after all.

Synonyms: Select the word or phrase whose meaning is closest to the word in capital letters.

1. REBUKE
   A. censure
   B. dither
   C. excise
   D. assuage
   E. conciliate

2. IRATE
   A. ashen
   B. pallid
   C. incensed
   D. wan
   E. alabaster

3. CONVICTION
   A. exposition
   B. mystification
   C. moroseness
   D. curriculum
   E. certitude

4. SALLOW
   A. pallid
   B. haggard
   C. vacillating
   D. livid
   E. incensed

Analogies: Select the answer choice that best completes the meaning of the sentence.

5. Admonished is to rebuked as
   A. censured is to dithered
   B. reprimanded is to ran amuck
   C. scolded is to mollified
   D. told off is to palliated
   E. reproached is to reproved

6. Vacillate is to nebulous as
   A. expose is to ambiguous
   B. infuse is to amorphous
   C. toll is to imprecise
   D. waver is to muddled
   E. empty is to tenuous

Sentence Completions: Choose the word or words that, when inserted in the sentence, <u>best</u> fits the meaning of the sentence as a whole.

7. Desiree feared letting her mind _____; she knew that thinking obsessively about the infuriating situation would only make her more _____.
   A. dither . . livid
   B. run amuck . . irate
   C. waver . . incensed
   D. compel . . sure
   E. exasperate . . psychic

8. Lorenzo had absolute conviction that he would win the election; this _____ made his opponents fear foul play.
   A. certitude
   B. exposition
   C. curriculum
   D. monotone
   E. grimace

1. **A.** *Rebuke* means *scold harshly.* Choice A, *censure,* means *scold harshly in an official way,* like by a court, and is the best answer. *Dither* means *be unsure, excise* means *remove,* and *assuage* and *conciliate* mean *soothe.*

2. **C.** *Irate* and *incensed* mean *very angry. Ashen, pallid, wan,* and *alabaster* all mean *white* or *pale.*

3. **E.** *Conviction* and *certitude* mean *sureness. Exposition* means *explanation, mystification* means *confusion, moroseness* means *sadness,* and *curriculum* means *plan of study.*

4. **A.** *Sallow* means *pale.* Choice B, *haggard,* does not work as well as Choice A, *pallid. Haggard* means *tired,* and might make someone pale, but *pallid* is a synonym for *sallow.*

5. **E.** "Admonished (scolded) is less strong than rebuked (scolded strongly)."
   - A. Censured (scolded strongly) is less strong than dithered (was unsure) . . . no.
   - B. Reprimanded (scolded strongly) is less strong than ran amuck . . . no.
   - C. Scolded is less strong than mollified (soothed) . . . maybe, but they are not related in the same way as *admonished* and *rebuked.*
   - D. Told off is less strong than palliated (soothed) . . . maybe, but they are not related in the same way as *admonished* and *rebuked.*
   - (E.) Reproached (scolded) is less strong than reproved (scolded strongly) . . . yes!

   Remember to try all the choices!

6. **D.** "A person might vacillate (waver) about something nebulous (unclear)."
   - A. A person might expose about something ambiguous (unclear) . . . no.
   - B. A person might infuse (mix) about something amorphous (unclear) . . . no.
   - C. A person might toll (ring) about something imprecise (unclear) . . . no.
   - (D.) A person might waver about something muddled (unclear) . . . yes.
   - E. A person might empty about something tenuous (unclear) . . . no.

7. **B.** "Desiree feared letting her mind <u>get obsessive</u>; she knew that thinking obsessively about the infuriating situation would only make her more <u>infuriated</u>."

   Choice B works best. *Run amuck* means *be out of control,* and *irate* means *very angry.*

8. **A.** "Lorenzo had absolute conviction that he would win the election; this <u>conviction</u> made his opponents fear foul play."

   Certitude and *conviction* mean *sureness.*

Group 14
Affable Jake

Find each of the following words on the *New Moon* page number provided. Based on the way each word is used in the book, guess at its definition.

1. **Impaired** (p. 126) might mean _____

   _____

2. **Kismet** (p. 126) might mean _____

   _____

3. **Dilapidated** (p. 126) might mean _____

   _____

4. **Affably** (p. 129) might mean _____

   _____

5. **Corresponding** (p. 131) might mean _____

   _____

6. **Stand** (p. 133) might mean _____

   _____

7. **Brawny** (p. 139) might mean _____

   _____

8. **Impish** (p. 139) might mean _____

   _____

56 Let's see how you did. Check your answers, write the exact definitions, and reread the sentence in *New Moon* where each word appears. Then complete the drills on the next page.

1. **Impaired** (p. 126) means *weakened.*

2. **Kismet** (p. 126) means *fate,* something "meant to be."

3. **Dilapidated** (p. 126) means *run-down.* Synonyms: decrepit, ramshackle.

4. **Affably** (p. 129) means *in a friendly way.* Synonyms: amiably, congenially, genially. OK, *New Moon* Quiz 2. Look at the list of characters below. Who treats whom affably?

   Edward, Jacob, Mike, Jessica, Angela, Lauren, Rosalie, Charlie.

   Let's try it again, but this time who is not so affable to whom? (Sorry Lauren, but you deserve it.)

5. **Corresponding** (p. 131) means *matching.* Do you remember where you last heard this word? In geometry, when a pair of parallel lines is crossed by another line, two sets of angles form. In these two sets, angles that are in matching locations are called *corresponding.* Sorry to bring up geometry.

6. **Stand** (p. 133) in this case means *grouping.* Of course, it can also mean *being on one's feet* or *a table that holds something.* This is another perfect example of a word with several meanings that the SAT, ACT, GED, or SSAT might use in a reading comprehension question.

7. **Brawny** (p. 139) means *strong and muscular.* This reminds me of Brawny paper towels. You've seen the commercials—"the strength of Brawny." The older commercials also featured a giant lumberjack with a deep voice and massive muscles. He looked a lot like Emmett actually. If you are ever stumped by a word, ask yourself if you've ever seen or heard the word anywhere: in Spanish class, in a movie, as the name of a restaurant, or even as the name of a product. Synonym: burly.

8. **Impish** (p. 139) means *playful* or *mischievous,* like an *imp* (a mischievous creature of myths).

Synonyms: Select the word or phrase whose meaning is closest to the word in capital letters.

1. DILAPIDATED
   A. impaired
   B. kismet
   C. genial
   D. decrepit
   E. brawny

2. AFFABLE
   A. amiable
   B. impish
   C. irate
   D. livid
   E. incensed

3. CORRESPOND
   A. match
   B. stand
   C. run amuck
   D. rebuke
   E. reproach

4. BRAWNY
   A. sallow
   B. tentative
   C. haggard
   D. muscular
   E. grotesque

Analogies: Select the answer choice that best completes the meaning of the sentence.

5. Stand is to trees as
   A. birds are to a flock
   B. pack is to vampires
   C. coven is to vampires
   D. dilapidated is to motorcycles
   E. impish is to imps

6. Impish is to serious as
   A. impaired is to weakened
   B. affable is to hostile
   C. dilapidated is to ramshackle
   D. amiable is to genial
   E. nebulous is to ambiguous

Sentence Completions: Choose the word that, when inserted in the sentence, <u>best</u> fits the meaning of the sentence as a whole.

7. Mike expected the auditors to be cold and indifferent and was surprised by their _____ demeanor.
   A. callous
   B. incensed
   C. affable
   D. dithering
   E. palliated

8. Charlotte found that no matter how hard she hit the ball, Allie seemed to hit it back with _____ strength, matching her shot for shot.
   A. tennis
   B. ravenous
   C. petulant
   D. corresponding
   E. mollified

1. **D.** *Dilapidated* and *decrepit* mean *run-down*. *Impaired* means *weakened, kismet* means *fate, genial* means *friendly,* and *brawny* means *strong.*

2. **A.** *Affable* and *amiable* both mean *friendly. Impish* means *playful. Irate, livid,* and *incensed* mean *very angry.*

3. **A.** *Correspond* means *match. Stand* can mean *group, run amuck* means *be out of control,* and *rebuke* and *reproach* mean *scold.*

4. **D.** *Brawny* means *strong and muscular. Sallow* means *pale, tentative* means *hesitant, haggard* means *tired looking,* and *grotesque* means *very disgusting.*

5. **C.** "A stand is a group of trees."
   - A. Birds are a group of a flock . . . no, but if this choice said "a flock is a group of birds," it would be a perfect answer. Sometimes the SSAT reverses the words. That's easy to catch now that you know to watch for it!
   - B. A pack is a group of vampires . . . no way, a *pack* is a group of *wolves.* You'll know all about that pretty soon . . .
   - C. A coven is a group of vampires . . . yes.
   - D. Dilapidated is a group of motorcycles . . . not necessarily.
   - E. Impish is a group of imps . . . no.

6. **B.** "Impish (playful) is the opposite of serious."
   - A. Impaired is the opposite of weakened . . . no, they are synonyms.
   - B. Affable (friendly) is the opposite of hostile (unfriendly) . . . yes!
   - C. Dilapidated is the opposite of ramshackle . . . no, they both mean *run-down.*
   - D. Amiable is the opposite of genial . . . no, they both mean *friendly.*
   - E. Nebulous is the opposite of ambiguous . . . no, they both mean *unclear.*

7. **C.** "Mike expected the auditors to be cold and indifferent and was surprised by their _warm_ demeanor."

   The only evidence in the sentence is that the auditors were the opposite of "cold and indifferent," so *affable* (warm and friendly) is the best choice.

8. **D.** "Charlotte found that no matter how hard she hit the ball, Allie seemed to hit it back with _matching_ strength, matching her shot for shot."

   Corresponding means *matching.* Be careful of a choice like *tennis,* which is related to hitting a ball back and forth, but does not work to fill the blank. That's why you think of a word you want before you look at the choices.

Group 15
Perquisites

Find each of the following words on the *New Moon* page number provided. Based on the way each word is used in the book, guess at its definition.

1. **Bane** (p. 140) might mean _____

   _____

2. **Perk** (p. 147) might mean _____

   _____

3. **Reparable** (p. 157) might mean _____

   _____

4. **Tangible** (p. 161) might mean _____

   _____

5. **Infiltrated** (p. 161) might mean _____

   _____

6. **Marveling** (p. 164) might mean _____

   _____

7. **Aberrant** (p. 165) might mean _____

   _____

8. **Exuberant** (p. 167) might mean _____

   _____

Let's see how you did. Check your answers, write the exact definitions, and reread the sentence in *New Moon* where each word appears. Then complete the drills on the next page.

Definitions

1. **Bane** (p. 140) means *burden* or *curse.* Sometimes you can get a sense whether a word is positive or negative just by hearing it, and *bane* certainly does not sound good. In fact, "bane" is the name of a Batman villain, a poisonous plant, and the character taken over by Agent Smith in *The Matrix.* If you think that a word sounds negative, trust yourself, because you're probably right.

2. **Perk** (p. 147) means *benefit.* That's pretty easy, and you probably know this word already, but I included it here because *perk* is short for the word *perquisite,* which I've seen stump tons of students on the SAT. When you're not sure of the meaning of a word, think of other words that it reminds you of.

3. **Reparable** (p. 157) means exactly what it sounds like, *repairable.* Synonyms: rectifiable, salvageable.

4. **Tangible** (p. 161) means *touchable* or *real.*

5. **Infiltrated** (p. 161) means *entered.* Often this word implies that someone entered secretly, like in *Family Guy* when Stewie says, "Bertram's obviously been planning this attack for some time, but what's his master plan? I must find out! Therefore, I have no choice but to shrink myself down, and **infiltrate** his lair." (Fox, *Family Guy,* "Emission Impossible," 2001) Do you remember where that lair is located? LOL.

6. **Marveling** (p. 164) means *with **amazement.***

7. **Aberrant** (p. 165) means *abnormal.* Synonyms: anomalous, atypical, deviant, divergent.

8. **Exuberant** (p. 167) means *psyched* (very excited). Synonyms: buoyant, ebullient, ecstatic, elated, euphoric, exultant, jubilant, rapturous.

Synonyms: Select the word or phrase whose meaning is closest to the word in capital letters.

1. BANE
   A. kismet
   B. stand
   C. curse
   D. imp
   E. marvel

2. PERQUISITE
   A. benefit
   B. exposition
   C. curriculum
   D. precipice
   E. crag

3. TANGIBLE
   A. buoyant
   B. ebullient
   C. elated
   D. euphoric
   E. touchable

4. ABERRANT
   A. reparable
   B. rectifiable
   C. salvageable
   D. anomalous
   E. rapturous

Analogies: Select the answer choice that best completes the meaning of the sentence.

5. Morose is to exuberant as
   A. reparable is to salvageable
   B. tangible is to real
   C. glum is to jubilant
   D. affable is to amiable
   E. dilapidated is to decrepit

6. Perk is to bane as
   A. authoritative is to imperious
   B. constant is to vacillating
   C. melodramatic is to histrionic
   D. solicitous is to concerned
   E. piqued is to irritated

Sentence Completions: Choose the word that, when inserted in the sentence, best fits the meaning of the sentence as a whole.

7. Bilbo surreptitiously approached the trolls looking for a way to _____ their group and pick their pockets.
   A. steal
   B. infiltrate
   C. correspond
   D. rebuke
   E. reproach

8. The lawyer sought _____ proof that could permanently free his client of blame.
   A. reparable
   B. dilapidated
   C. congenial
   D. corresponding
   E. tangible

1. **C.** Bane means *curse. Kismet* means *destiny, stand* can mean *group, imp* is a *mischievous creature,* and *marvel* can mean *something amazing.*

2. **A.** *Perquisite* means *benefit,* like a perk. *Exposition* means *explanation, curriculum* means *plan of study,* and *precipice* and *crag* mean *cliff.*

3. **E.** *Tangible* means *touchable. Buoyant, ebullient, elated,* and *euphoric* mean *psyched.*

4. **D.** *Aberrant* and *anomalous* mean *abnormal.* If you're not sure of the answer, use the process of elimination—cross off answers that you are **sure** don't work and choose the best of what's left. *Reparable, rectifiable,* and *salvageable* mean *repairable,* like Bella's motorcycle, thanks to Jacob. *Rapturous* means *psyched.*

5. **C.** "Morose (sad) is the opposite of exuberant (psyched)."
   A. Reparable is the opposite of salvageable . . . no, they both mean *repairable.*
   B. Tangible is the opposite of real . . . no, they are synonyms.
   C. Glum (sad) is the opposite of jubilant (psyched) . . . yes.
   D. Affable is the opposite of amiable . . . no, they both mean *friendly.*
   E. Dilapidated is the opposite of decrepit . . . no, they both mean *run-down.*

6. **B.** "Perk is the opposite of bane (burden)."
   Look at all these great words that you've learned!
   A. Authoritative (commanding) is the opposite of imperious (bossy) . . . no.
   B. Constant is the opposite of vacillating (wavering) . . . yes!
   C. Melodramatic is the opposite of histrionic (melodramatic) . . . no.
   D. Solicitous (concerned) is the opposite of concerned . . . no.
   E. Piqued (irritated) is the opposite of irritated . . . no.

7. **B.** "Bilbo surreptitiously approached the trolls looking for a way to *enter* their group and pick their pockets."
   Infiltrate means *enter.* Be careful of a choice like *steal,* which is related to "picking pockets," but does not work to fill the blank. Again, that's why you think of a word you want before you look at the choices.

8. **E.** "The lawyer sought *solid* proof that could permanently free his client of blame."
   Tangible means *real* or *touchable* and is the best answer.

Quiz 3

I. Let's review some of the words that you've seen in Groups 11–15. Match each of the following words to the correct definition or synonym on the right. Then check the solutions on page 171.

1. Morose		A. Flat and dull
2. Monotone		B. Conciliated
3. Comity		C. Amorphous
4. Mollified		D. Gloomy
5. Haggard		E. Certitude
6. Nebulous		F. Group of nations
7. Rebuke		G. Reprove
8. Conviction		H. Blanched
9. Sallow		I. Tired looking
10. Affable		J. Decrepit
11. Brawny		K. Euphoric
12. Dilapidated		L. Benefit
13. Perquisite		M. Anomalous
14. Aberrant		N. Burly
15. Exuberant		O. Amiable

II. Let's review several of the word parts that you've seen in Groups 11–15. Match each of the following word parts to the correct definition or synonym on the right. Then check the solutions on page 171.

16. Mono-		A. Against
17. Solo-		B. Together
18. Com-		C. Join
19. Anti-		D. One
20. -Fuse		E. Disease or treatment
21. Path-		F. Alone

Diversions

Find each of the following words on the *New Moon* page number provided. Based on the way each word is used in the book, guess at its definition.

1. **Atone** (p. 167) might mean _____

   _____

2. **Interspersed** (p. 168) might mean _____

   _____

3. **Implications** (p. 168) might mean _____

   _____

4. **Glacial** (p. 172) might mean _____

   _____

5. **Divert** (p. 174) might mean _____

   _____

6. **Tempo** (p. 177) might mean _____

   _____

7. **Albino** (p. 179) might mean _____

   _____

8. **Contorting** (p. 182) might mean _____

   _____

Let's see how you did. Check your answers, write the exact definitions, and reread the sentence in *New Moon* where each word appears. Then complete the drills on the next page.

1. **Atone** (p. 167) means *make up for* or *pay back*. Synonyms: expiate, recompense, redress.

2. **Interspersed** (p. 168) means *scattered* or *dispersed among*. *Inter-* means *among* or *between,* as in **inter**murals (matches **between** schools). Incidentally, *intra-* means *within,* as in **intra**murals (matches played by teams **within** the school). So, if you went to Forks High School, you'd play **inter**mural matches against players from other schools, maybe Embry, Quil, and Jake from La Push; and you'd play **intra**mural matches against players from **within** Forks, maybe Mike, Angela, and Ben.

3. **Implications** (p. 168) means *hinted meanings.* It comes from the word *imply.*

4. **Glacial** (p. 172) means *icy.* In fact, *glace* means *ice* in French. *Glacial* can refer literally to cold temperatures or figuratively to the "cold shoulder."

5. **Divert** (p. 174) means *steer away.* It can also mean *entertain,* as in the Spanish verb *divirtirse* (to enjoy), and the great SAT word *diversion,* which means *recreation.* Here's the connection: **recreation**, **entertainment,** and fun **steer** you **away** from seriousness or worries.

6. **Tempo** (p. 177) means *speed* or *pace,* and comes from the Latin word *tempus,* meaning *time.* That helps you remember challenging words like *temporize* (delay, stall for time) and *temporal* (relating to time).

7. **Albino** (p. 179) refers to *a person with white skin and hair.* Notice how often Bella is described as pale or white. Remember anyone else who is pale and white? I'm just saying . . .

8. **Contorting** (p. 182) means *twisting* or *knotting up.* Contortionists twist their bodies into unbelievable shapes. Check out "Cirque du Soleil contortionists" on YouTube for some startling clips.

Synonyms: Select the word or phrase whose meaning is closest to the word in capital letters.

1. ATONE
   A. waver
   B. wallow
   C. pique
   D. expiate
   E. temporize

2. GLACIAL
   A. rectifiable
   B. tangible
   C. aberrant
   D. cold
   E. atypical

3. DIVERSION
   A. recreation
   B. perquisite
   C. bane
   D. remorse
   E. tempo

4. CONTORT
   A. relent
   B. cease
   C. twist
   D. toll
   E. ape

Analogies: Select the answer choice that best completes the meaning of the sentence.

5. Expiate is to recompense as
   A. infiltrate is to correspond
   B. rebuke is to dither
   C. atone is to redress
   D. admonish is to vacillate
   E. censure is to waver

6. Albino is to interspersed as
   A. implied is to blanched
   B. alabaster is to scattered
   C. exultant is to jubilant
   D. elated is to ecstatic
   E. vampires is to amber

Sentence Completions: Choose the word that, when inserted in the sentence, <u>best</u> fits the meaning of the sentence as a whole.

7. Mike considered the implications of his supervisor's _____ demeanor; was she angry or just unfriendly?
   A. diverting
   B. contorted
   C. impaired
   D. dilapidated
   E. glacial

8. Several tall oaks were _____ among a stand of spruce trees.
   A. excised
   B. interspersed
   C. sallow
   D. affable
   E. amiable

1. **D.** *Atone* and *expiate* mean *make up for. Wallow* means *immerse oneself in, pique* means *irritate,* and *temporize* means *delay.*
2. **D.** *Glacial* means *cold. Rectifiable* means *fixable, tangible* means *touchable,* and *aberrant* and *atypical* mean *unusual.* A- means *not,* as in *amoral* and *apathetic,* so *atypical* means *not typical—unusual.*
3. **A.** *Diversion* means *recreation. Perquisite* means *benefit,* like a perk; *bane* means *curse; remorse* means *regret;* and *tempo* means *pace.*
4. **C.** *Contort* means *twist. Relent* and *cease* are fabulous words for *end. Toll* means *ring,* and *ape* means *imitate.*
5. **C.** "Expiate is a synonym of recompense."
   - A. Infiltrate (enter) is a synonym of correspond (match) . . . no, that makes no sense.
   - B. Rebuke (scold) is a synonym of dither (waver) . . . no.
   - C. Atone is a synonym of redress . . . yes, they both mean *make up for.*
   - D. Admonish (scold) is a synonym of vacillate (waver) . . . no.
   - E. Censure (scold publicly) is a synonym of waver . . . no.
6. **B.** "Albino is to interspersed."

   Usually the two words in the question are directly related to each other, and the best strategy is to make a sentence that defines one with the other. However, occasionally on the SSAT, the two words are related not to each other but to the two words below. You can recognize this setup when the words in the question are totally unrelated. In that case, set up a relationship to the words below. Choice B is correct since *albino* means a person with *alabaster* (white) skin, and *interspersed* means *scattered.*
7. **E.** "Mike considered the implications of his supervisor's <u>*angry/ unfriendly*</u> demeanor; was she angry or just unfriendly?"

   Glacial means *cold* or *unfriendly.* Always choose an answer based on evidence in the question. In this case, you can refer to "angry" or "unfriendly."
8. **B.** "Several tall oaks were <u>*????*</u> among a stand of spruce trees."

   Interspersed means *scattered* and is the best answer.
   Occasionally, you might not be able to use a word from the sentence or even think of a word to fill the blank. If that happens, try the choices for the blank and use the process of elimination. Make sure the word fits the evidence in the sentence.

Group 17

Gruesome

Find each of the following words on the *New Moon* page number provided. Based on the way each word is used in the book, guess at its definition.

1. **Severe** (p. 186) might mean _____
   _____

2. **Coaxed** (p. 189) might mean _____
   _____

3. **Dire** (p. 190) might mean _____
   _____

4. **Pathetic** (p. 190) might mean _____
   _____

5. **Gruesome** (p. 190) might mean _____
   _____

6. **Clinically** (p. 191) might mean _____
   _____

7. **Impulsive** (p. 192) might mean _____
   _____

8. **Ironic** (p. 192) might mean _____
   _____

Let's see how you did. Check your answers, write the exact definitions,
and reread the sentence in *New Moon* where each word appears. Then
complete the drills on the next page.

1. **Severe** (p. 186) means *harsh.* Synonym: stern.

2. **Coaxed** (p. 189) means *urged* or *persuaded. Coax* was a synonym for
    prod in Group 10. The other synonyms were *cajole, enjoin, entreat,*
    exhort, goad, implore, incite, and *spur.*

3. **Dire** (p. 190) means *dangerous* or *serious.* Ten thousand years ago
    dire wolves roamed North America. They were five feet long and
    deadly. If they could have stood on two legs they would have
    towered over seven feet tall. Sound like anyone you know?

4. **Pathetic** (p. 190) means *pitiful* or *deserving pity.*

5. **Gruesome** (p. 190) means *horrible.* Interestingly, *horrible* actually
    means *causing horror. Gruesome* things, like blood drying in thick
    streaks across Bella's cheek and matting in her muddy hair, cause
    horror. Gruesome is pretty much a synonym for *grotesque* from Group
    12. Another great synonym is *grisly.*

6. **Clinically** (p. 191) means *scientifically* or *without emotion,* the way
    a doctor might behave in a clinic, like when Dr. House tells the
    crowd in a waiting room, "Hello, sick people and their loved
    ones! . . . In the interest of saving time and avoiding a lot of boring
    chitchat later, I'm Doctor Gregory House; you can call me 'Greg.'
    I'm one of three doctors staffing this **clinic** this morning." (Fox,
    House, M.D., "Occam's Razor," 2004)

7. **Impulsive** (p. 192) means *on an impulse* or *spontaneous.* Synonyms:
    hasty, impetuous, rash, unpremeditated.

8. **Ironic** (p. 192) means *happening in a different and disappointingly*
    funnier way than expected. Okay, here's the English class that you've
    always dreamed of. Let's discuss this scene from *New Moon.* Why
    does Bella say that *Jacob holding her hand while Dr. Snow stitches*
    her forehead is ironic? Let me know what you think. Share your
    opinion at www.DefiningTwilight.com/ironic. By the way, this
    is the type of question you'll see if you have to take the SAT
    Literature Subject Test. Although on that test you get to choose
    from multiple-choice answers.

Synonyms: Select the word or phrase whose meaning is closest to the word in capital letters.

1. SEVERE
   - A. callous
   - B. clinical
   - C. stern
   - D. impulsive
   - E. ironic

2. COAX
   - A. goad
   - B. atone
   - C. expiate
   - D. recompense
   - E. redress

3. PATHETIC
   - A. contorted
   - B. interspersed
   - C. dire
   - D. pitiful
   - E. clinical

4. GRUESOME
   - A. grisly
   - B. harsh
   - C. hasty
   - D. impetuous
   - E. rash

Analogies: Select the answer choice that best completes the meaning of the sentence.

5. Impulsive is to spontaneous as
   - A. impetuous is to unpremeditated
   - B. ironic is to clinical
   - C. grotesque is to pathetic
   - D. cajole is to dire
   - E. glacial is to diverting

6. Doctor is to clinical as
   - A. albino is to impulsive
   - B. prophet is to prescient
   - C. contortionist is to marveling
   - D. psychopath is to nebulous
   - E. vampire is to brawny

Sentence Completions: Choose the word that, when inserted in the sentence, <u>best</u> fits the meaning of the sentence as a whole.

7. Attendees of the convention thought it _____ that, even though it was spring, it snowed the entire week of the International Convention on Glacial Studies.
   - A. severe
   - B. dire
   - C. pathetic
   - D. hasty
   - E. ironic

8. To her friends' dismay, Brittany would attend only _____ movies filled with gruesome scenes.
   - A. ironic
   - B. pathetic
   - C. grotesque
   - D. aberrant
   - E. affable

1. **C.** *Severe* and *stern* both mean *harsh*. *Callous* means *insensitive*, *clinical* means *scientific*, *impulsive* means *spontaneous*, and *ironic* means *happening differently than expected*.

2. **A.** *Coax* and *goad* both mean *urge*. If you did not initially make the link to the word *goad*, then use the process of elimination. *Atone, expiate, recompense*, and *redress* mean *make up for.*

3. **D.** *Pathetic* means *pitiful*. *Contorted* means *twisted*, *interspersed* means *scattered*, and *dire* means *serious*.

4. **A.** *Gruesome* and *grisly* mean *horrible—causing horror*. *Harsh* means *rough*, not necessarily *horrible*. *Rash* (which means *impulsive*) can refer to *itchy red bumps on skin* which can be, but are not necessarily, horrible. The correct answer should match directly, without a lot of explanation.

5. **A.** "Impulsive means spontaneous."
   - (A.) Impetuous means unpremeditated . . . yes, they both mean *spontaneous.*
   - B . Ironic (incongruous) means clinical (scientific) . . . no.
   - C . Grotesque (horrible) means pathetic (pitiful) . . . no.
   - D. Cajole (urge) means dire (dangerous) . . . no.
   - E . Glacial (cold) means diverting (fun) . . . no.

6. **B.** "A doctor is clinical."
   - A . An albino (person with white skin) is impulsive (spontaneous) . . . not necessarily.
   - (B.) A prophet is prescient (prophetic—able to predict) . . . yes!
   - C . A contortionist is marveling . . . no, although spectators might marvel (be amazed).
   - D. A psychopath is nebulous (unclear) . . . maybe, but this is not as direct a relationship as choice B. A prophet is by definition able to predict; a psychopath may or may not be unclear.
   - E . A vampire is brawny . . . not necessarily; depends if you mean Emmett or Alice . . .

7. **E.** "Attendees of the convention thought it *surprising/funny* that, even though it was spring, it snowed the entire week of the International Convention on Glacial Studies."

   Ironic means *happening in a different and disappointingly funnier way than expected*. Several answers might seem to work, but choose the answer most supported by evidence in the passage: snow during a conference on glacial studies during spring is *surprising and funny*, but not necessarily *dire* (dangerous), *pathetic* (pitiful), or *hasty* (rushed).

8. **C.** "To her friends' dismay, Brittany would attend only *gruesome* movies filled with gruesome scenes."

   Grotesque and *gruesome* mean *horrible*.

Group 18
Less Potent Nightmares

Find each of the following words on the *New Moon* page number provided. Based on the way each word is used in the book, guess at its definition.

1. **Potency** (p. 193) might mean _____

   _____

2. **Edict** (p. 193) might mean _____

   _____

3. **Virtues** (p. 194) might mean _____

   _____

4. **Mutated** (p. 194) might mean _____

   _____

5. **Topographical** (p. 196) might mean _____

   _____

6. **Cataclysmic** (p. 201) might mean _____

   _____

7. **Entail** (p. 202) might mean _____

   _____

8. **Foiled** (p. 204) might mean _____

   _____

Let's see how you did. Check your answers, write the exact definitions, and reread the sentence in *New Moon* where each word appears. Then complete the drills on the next page.

1. **Potency** (p. 193) means *strength.*

2. **Edict** (p. 193) means *formal declaration.* Two of the most important edicts of all time: 1) the Edict of Milan in which the Roman Empire stated that it would be neutral with regard to religious worship, and 2) the Volturi Edict of 2006 in which Aro decreed that since Bella knows of the existence of vampires, she must be . . . well, I won't spoil it for you in case you haven't read that far yet! Synonyms: decree, fiat, mandate, proclamation.

3. **Virtues** (p. 194) means *good qualities.* The opposite of *virtue* is *vice,* a bad quality.

4. **Mutated** (p. 194) means *genetically changed,* that's why the superhumans in the X-Men comics are called mutants—they have had genetic changes that give them special powers. In the television show *Heroes*, Mohinder Suresh thinks genetic **mutation** is also responsible for Claire, Hiro, Nathan, and Peter's special abilities.

5. **Topographical** (p. 196) means *showing physical features, such as elevation.* This is a very cool word to break apart. *Topo-* means *place,* and *graph* refers to *writing,* so *topography* is *writing about a place,* like on a map!

6. **Cataclysmic** (p. 201) means *disastrous.* This reminds me of *dire* from Group 17. Synonyms: calamitous, catastrophic.

7. **Entail** (p. 202) means *involve.*

8. **Foiled** (p. 204) means *defeated.* Villains in movies often use this word when defeated, such as when sinister villain Sideshow Bob complains about Bart, "The spirited little scamp who twice **foiled** my evil schemes and sent me to this dank . . . " (Fox, *The Simpsons,* "Cape Feare," 1993) Synonyms: stymied, thwarted.

Synonyms: Select the word or phrase whose meaning is closest to the word in capital letters.

1. POTENT
   A. dire
   B. strong
   C. foiled
   D. defeated
   E. unpremeditated

2. EDICT
   A. mandate
   B. catastrophe
   C. virtue
   D. perquisite
   E. exuberance

3. MUTATED
   A. entailed
   B. involved
   C. cajoled
   D. changed
   E. goaded

4. CATACLYSMIC
   A. catastrophic
   B. potent
   C. pathetic
   D. clinical
   E. ironic

Analogies: Select the answer choice that best completes the meaning of the sentence.

5. Virtuous is to good as
   A. mollified is to exposed
   B. infused is to separated
   C. grotesque is to pleasant
   D. haggard is to robust
   E. nebulous is to unclear

6. Topographical is to map as
   A. impasse is to passageway
   B. precipice is to contingency
   C. tawny is to color
   D. trio is to convalescence
   E. aversion is to basilisk

Sentence Completions: Choose the word or words that, when inserted in the sentence, <u>best</u> fits the meaning of the sentence as a whole.

7. After crops were severely damaged from the high winds and heavy rains, farmers feared that additional _____ weather could have _____ effects.
   A. stern . . mutating
   B. topographical . . calamitous
   C. potent . . foiling
   D. impetuous . . dire
   E. harsh . . catastrophic

8. Velma knew that in order to _____ the thief, she would have to infiltrate his hideout just before twilight, defeating him before he even set out for the night.
   A. placate
   B. admonish
   C. foil
   D. mutate
   E. marvel at

1. **B.** *Potent* means *strong.* Watch out for choice A, *dire* (dangerous). A dire wolf is *strong,* but *dire* does not directly mean *strong.* *Foiled* means *defeated. Unpremeditated* means *spontaneous* and is an interesting word to break apart. *Un-* means *not,* *pre-* means *before,* and *meditate* means *contemplate,* so *unpremeditated* means *not contemplated beforehand—spontaneous!*

2. **A.** *Edict* and *mandate* mean *formal declaration. Catastrophe* means *disaster, virtue* means *good quality, perquisite* means *benefit,* and *exuberance* means *excitement.*

3. **D.** *Mutated* means *changed. Entailed* means *involved,* and *cajoled* and *goaded* mean *urged.*

4. **A.** *Cataclysmic* and *catastrophic* mean *disastrous. Potent* means *strong, pathetic* means *pitiable, clinical* means *scientific,* and *ironic* means *surprising and humorous.*

5. **E.** "Virtuous means good."
   A. Mollified (soothed) means exposed . . . no.
   B. Infused (mixed) means separated . . . no.
   C. Grotesque (gross) means pleasant . . . no.
   D. Haggard (tired) means robust . . . no.
   E. Nebulous (unclear) means unclear . . . yes!

6. **C.** "Topographical is a type of map."
   A. Impasse is a type of passageway . . . no, *impasse* is a *dead end.*
   B. Precipice (cliff) is a type of contingency (possibility) . . . no.
   C. Tawny is a type of color . . . yes, *tawny* is *yellowish-brown.*
   D. Trio (group of three) is a type of convalescence (healing) . . . no, that makes no sense.
   E. Aversion (avoidance) is a type of basilisk (legendary creature) . . . no.

7. **E.** "After crops were severely damaged from the high winds and heavy rains, farmers feared that additional <u>severe</u> weather could have <u>damaging</u> effects."
   Questions with two blanks are actually easier than questions with one blank—you have two opportunities to use the process of elimination. So think of a word to fill each bank and then use the process of elimination, one blank at a time. *Harsh* means *severe,* and *catastrophic* means *disastrous.*

8. **C.** "Velma knew that in order to <u>defeat</u> the thief, she would have to infiltrate his hideout just before twilight, defeating him before he even set out for the night."
   Foil means *defeat.*

Another Abrupt Departure

Find each of the following words on the *New Moon* page number provided. Based on the way each word is used in the book, guess at its definition.

1. **Capitulation** (p. 206) might mean _____

   _____

2. **Petulance** (p. 208) might mean _____

   _____

3. **Carnage** (p. 211) might mean _____

   _____

4. **Crescent** (p. 214) might mean _____

   _____

5. **Malevolent** (p. 215) might mean _____

   _____

6. **Defiled** (p. 216) might mean _____

   _____

7. **Parched** (p. 222) might mean _____

   _____

8. **Abrupt** (p. 223) might mean _____

   _____

Let's see how you did. Check your answers, write the exact definitions, and reread the sentence in *New Moon* where each word appears. Then complete the drills on the next page.

1. **Capitulation** (p. 206) means *surrender.* A few lines before, Bella says, "I'm giving up . . . " *Capitulation* refers to "giving up," and that's exactly what it means. You can almost always figure out a tough word by looking at the context! Synonyms for *capitulate:* cede, concede, relent, yield.

2. **Petulance** (p. 208) means *irritability.* I examined this word in *Defining Twilight,* but I couldn't resist including it again; I've seen it stump too many students on the SAT and ACT. Synonyms: peevishness, sullenness.

3. **Carnage** (p. 211) means *slaughter* or *massacre. Carn-* means *flesh,* as in *carnivorous* (flesh eating), and *-age* can mean *lots of,* so *carnage* is **lots of flesh** *chopped up*—gross! As Jacob says, "You sure can pick them, Bella."

4. **Crescent** (p. 214) means *half-moon–shaped,* like Pillsbury Crescent Rolls, and like the shape of the new moon. Synonyms: lunette, lunula.

5. **Malevolent** (p. 215) means *very hostile* or *wanting to harm.* This word even sounds harmful, like the word *violent.* Synonyms: abominable, baleful, execrable, loathsome, maleficent, malicious, odious, rancorous, venomous. Why do we have so many *violent* synonyms?

6. **Defiled** (p. 216) means *contaminated.* Synonyms: befouled, marred, sullied, tainted.

7. **Parched** (p. 222) means *very dry* or *very thirsty.* Synonyms: arid, dehydrated, desiccated.

8. **Abrupt** (p. 223) in this case means *brief and rude.* Synonyms: blunt, brusque, curt, laconic, terse.

Synonyms: Select the word or phrase whose meaning is closest to the word in capital letters.

1. CAPITULATE
   A. defile
   B. parch
   C. relent
   D. mutate
   E. stymie

2. PETULANT
   A. sullen
   B. lunula
   C. lunette
   D. venomous
   E. loathsome

3. MALEVOLENT
   A. maleficent
   B. dehydrated
   C. desiccated
   D. parched
   E. curt

4. PARCHED
   A. potent
   B. virtuous
   C. topographical
   D. calamitous
   E. arid

Analogies: Select the answer choice that best completes the meaning of the sentence.

5. Carnage is to gruesome as
   A. capitulation is to crescent
   B. petulance is to defiled
   C. vampire is to malevolent
   D. slaughter is to grisly
   E. massacre is to parched

6. Toxins is to contamination as
   A. crescents is to befouling
   B. impurities is to sullying
   C. edicts is to marring
   D. kismet is to tainting
   E. infusions is to cleaning

Sentence Completions: Choose the word or words that, when inserted in the sentence, <u>best</u> fits the meaning of the sentence as a whole.

7. The singer was renowned for her _____ attitude; she was grumpy to staff and difficult to work with.
   A. capitulating
   B. solicitous
   C. petulant
   D. parched
   E. tentative

8. Hollywood insiders consider Josh Weinstein more _____ than _____; he is brusque but not as malicious as his reputation indicates.
   A. curt .. kind
   B. blunt .. malevolent
   C. defiled .. abominable
   D. crescent .. venomous
   E. laconic .. arid

1. **C.** *Capitulate* means *surrender*. *Relent* means *end* and is the best answer. *Defile* means *contaminate, parch* means *dry, mutate* means *change,* and *stymie* means *prevent*.

2. **A.** *Petulant* and *sullen* mean *irritable,* like Lauren. *Lunula* and *lunette* mean *half-moon–shaped*. *Venomous* and *loathsome* mean *very hostile*. The word *venomous* also means *having venom,* like a poisonous snake, or a poisonous vampire for that matter.

3. **A.** *Malevolent* and *maleficent* mean *very hostile*. *Dehydrated, desiccated,* and *parched* mean *very dry*. *Curt* means *brief and rude*.

4. **E.** *Parched* and *arid* mean *very dry*. When you don't know a word, see if you can relate it to anything you've ever heard of, such as a song, a movie, a book, a product, anything. The word *arid* reminds me of Arrid Extra Dry deodorant. That's enough to tell you that *arid* must be related to *extra dry!*

5. **D.** "Carnage (slaughter) looks gruesome (gross)."
   - A. Capitulation (surrender) looks crescent (half-moon–shaped) . . . no.
   - B. Petulance (irritability) looks defiled (contaminated) . . . no.
   - C. A vampire looks malevolent (very hostile) . . . come on, not all vampires look hostile, so how could you choose this one; at least look at the color of their eyes before you judge them!
   - (D.) Slaughter looks grisly (gross) . . . definitely.
   - E. Massacre looks parched (very dry) . . . no.

6. **B.** "Toxins cause contamination."
   - A. Crescents (half-moon shapes) cause befouling (contamination) . . . no.
   - (B.) Impurities cause sullying (contamination) . . . yes.
   - C. Edicts (formal declarations) cause marring (contamination) . . . no.
   - D. Kismet (fate) causes tainting (contamination) . . . no.
   - E. Infusions (mixtures) cause cleaning . . . no.

7. **C.** "The singer was renowned for her *grumpy/difficult* attitude; she was grumpy to staff and difficult to work with."
   Petulant means *irritable* and fits perfectly. Did you remember *solicitous* from Group 8? It's a terrific SAT and ACT word that means *interested* or *concerned*.

8. **B.** "Hollywood insiders consider Josh Weinstein more *brusque* than *malicious;* he is brusque but not as malicious as his reputation indicates."
   Brusque and *blunt* mean *brief and rude*. *Malicious* and *malevolent* mean *very hostile*. This is a common SAT sentence completion setup; the two blanks are defined in order in the second part of the sentence.

Group 20

James's Coven

Find each of the following words on the *New Moon* page number provided. Based on the way each word is used in the book, guess at its definition.

1. **Infectious** (p. 227) might mean _____

   _____

2. **Perforated** (p. 229) might mean _____

   _____

3. **Abyss** (p. 234) might mean _____

   _____

4. **Coven** (p. 236) might mean _____

   _____

5. **Quarry** (p. 236) might mean _____

   _____

6. **Compunctions** (p. 236) might mean _____

   _____

7. **Elated** (p. 236) might mean _____

   _____

8. **Eternity** (p. 237) might mean _____

   _____

Let's see how you did. Check your answers, write the exact definitions, and reread the sentence in *New Moon* where each word appears. Then complete the drills on the next page.

1. **Infectious** (p. 227) means *contagious.* Let's turn back to our petulant friend Dr. Gregory House for his thoughts on the subject: "**Infectious** or environmental . . . all we have to do is check out parasites, viruses, bacteria, fungi, prions, radiation, toxins, chemicals, . . . " (Fox, *House, M.D.,* "Fools for Love," 2004) Synonyms: communicable, transferable, transmittable.

2. **Perforated** (p. 229) means *pierced* or *with holes,* like the paper in your spiral notebook. Bella is referring back to the previous page, "The **hole** in my chest was worse than ever."

3. **Abyss** (p. 234) means *deep or bottomless pit.* This is one of those nature words that the SSAT loves to use. Synonyms: chasm, void. You saw *void* in Group 6 as a synonym for *devoid,* meaning *empty*— like *a bottomless pit.*

4. **Coven** (p. 236) means *group of vampires (or witches).* It actually comes from the word *convene* (to meet).

5. **Quarry** (p. 236) means *something hunted or pursued.* It can, of course, also refer to *a pit where gold or other minerals are mined.* Synonym: prey.

6. **Compunctions** (p. 236) means *regrets.* This was a synonym for *remorse* in Group 7. The other synonyms were *contrition, penitence, repentance,* and *ruefulness.* You can also add *qualms* and *scruples.*

7. **Elated** (p. 236) means *very psyched.* This is a great synonym for *exuberant* from Group 15. The other synonyms were *buoyant, ebullient, ecstatic, euphoric, exultant, jubilant,* and *rapturous.*

8. **Eternity** (p. 237) means *very long or endless time.* Synonym: perpetuity (from the word *perpetual*).

Synonyms: Select the word or phrase whose meaning is closest to the word in capital letters.

1. INFECTIOUS
   A. perforated
   B. contrite
   C. communicable
   D. rapturous
   E. blunt

2. ABYSS
   A. carnage
   B. chasm
   C. capitulation
   D. fiat
   E. edict

3. COMPUNCTION
   A. petulance
   B. peevishness
   C. potency
   D. virtues
   E. remorse

4. ELATED
   A. pathetic
   B. impulsive
   C. unpremeditated
   D. aberrant
   E. exuberant

Analogies: Select the answer choice that best completes the meaning of the sentence.

5. Hunter is to quarry as
   A. psychopath is to eternity
   B. vampire is to chicken
   C. albino is to chasm
   D. archaeologist is to artifact
   E. contortionist is to compunction

6. Eternity is to perpetual as
   A. infectious is to transferable
   B. perforated is to ecstatic
   C. coven is to euphoric
   D. bane is to jubilant
   E. perquisite is to exultant

Sentence Completions: Choose the word that, when inserted in the sentence, best fits the meaning of the sentence as a whole.

7. Classmates had never seen Jahira so _____ and wondered what was responsible for her sudden high spirits.
   A. stymied
   B. buoyant
   C. malicious
   D. impetuous
   E. melancholic

8. Vince fell deep into a(n) _____, his heart heavy after he discovered that Mandy had moved on and was engaged.
   A. elation
   B. eternity
   C. coven
   D. quarry
   E. abyss

1. **C.** *Infectious* means *contagious.* That's also what *communicable* means, like it can be **communicated** from one person to another. *Perforated* means *with holes, contrite* means *regretful, rapturous* means *very excited,* and *blunt* means *brief and rude.*

2. **B.** *Abyss* and *chasm* mean *deep or bottomless pit. Carnage* means *slaughter, capitulation* means *surrender,* and *fiat* and *edict* mean *formal declaration.*

3. **E.** *Compunction* means *regret.* That's also what *remorse* means. *Petulance* and *peevishness* mean *irritability, potency* means *strength,* and *virtues* means *good qualities.*

4. **E.** *Elated* and *exuberant* mean *very excited.* Use the process of elimination—cross off answers that you are **sure** don't work and choose the best of what's left. *Pathetic* means *pitiful, impulsive* and *unpremeditated* mean *spontaneous,* and *aberrant* means *abnormal.*

5. **D.** "A hunter hunts for a quarry."
   - A. A psychopath hunts for an eternity (a very long time) . . . no, that sounds like the tagline for a horror movie, but is not the correct answer.
   - B. A vampire hunts for a chicken . . . no, chickens are too small and way too easy to catch, try grizzlies.
   - C. An albino (person with white skin) hunts for a chasm (deep pit) . . . no.
   - (D.) An archaeologist hunts for an artifact . . . yes!
   - E. A contortionist hunts for a compunction (regret) . . . no.

6. **A.** "Eternity (very long or endless time) means perpetual (ongoing)."
   - (A.) Infectious (contagious) means transferable (contagious) . . . yes!
   - B. Perforated (with holes) means ecstatic (very excited) . . . no.
   - C. Coven (vampire group) means euphoric (very excited) . . . no.
   - D. Bane (curse) means jubilant (very excited) . . . no.
   - E. Perquisite (benefit) means exultant (very excited) . . . no.

7. **B.** "Classmates had never seen Jahira so *in high spirits* and wondered what was responsible for her sudden high spirits."

   Buoyant means *excited* and is the best answer. *Stymied* means *stuck or prevented, malicious* means *hostile, impetuous* means *spontaneous,* and *melancholic* means *sad.*

8. **E.** "Vince fell deep into a(n) *heavyheartedness,* his heart heavy after he discovered that Mandy had moved on and was engaged."

   None of the choices match *heavyheartedness.* If that ever happens, try the choices for the blank, use the process of elimination, and choose the best fit. *Abyss* means *a deep pit* and fits better than the other choices.

Quiz 4

I. Let's review some of the words that you've seen in Groups 16–20. Match each of the following words to the correct definition or synonym on the right. Then check the solutions on page 171.

1. Atone		A.	Icy
2. Glacial		B.	Goad
3. Contort		C.	Impetuous
4. Coax		D.	Make amends
5. Dire		E.	Twist
6. Impulsive		F.	Strength
7. Potency		G.	Thwarted
8. Virtue		H.	Dangerous
9. Foiled		I.	Laconic
10. Capitulation		J.	Good quality
11. Carnage		K.	Chasm
12. Abrupt		L.	Contrition
13. Abyss		M.	Buoyant
14. Compunction		N.	Slaughter
15. Elated		O.	Surrender

II. Let's review several of the word parts that you've seen in Groups 16–20. Match each of the following word parts to the correct definition or synonym on the right. Then check the solutions on page 171.

16. A-, Un-		A.	Flesh
17. -Graph		B.	Place
18. Pre-		C.	Not
19. Carn-		D.	Writing
20. Topo-		E.	Lots of
21. -age		F.	Before

Review

Match each group of synonyms to its general meaning. Then check the solutions on page 171.

1. Ceaseless
   Incessant
   Relentless

   A. Unpredictable

2. Homage
   Paean
   Tribute

   B. Calm

3. Capricious
   Erratic
   Fickle
   Mercurial
   Vacillating

   C. Very hungry

4. Anarchy
   Bedlam
   Chaos
   Mayhem
   Pandemonium
   Turmoil

   D. Endless

5. Famished
   Gluttonous
   Insatiable
   Rapacious
   Ravenous
   Voracious

   E. Something that honors

6. Aplomb
   Composure
   Equanimity
   Poise
   Sangfroid
   Serenity
   Tranquility

   F. Disorder

Group 21

Canine?

Find each of the following words on the *New Moon* page number provided. Based on the way each word is used in the book, guess at its definition.

1. **Dismissively** (p. 238) might mean _____

   _____

2. **Hysteria** (p. 238) might mean _____

   _____

3. **Conspiratorially** (p. 239) might mean _____

   _____

4. **Blithely** (p. 240) might mean _____

   _____

5. **Serrated** (p. 240) might mean _____

   _____

6. **Placate** (p. 241) might mean _____

   _____

7. **Incisors** (p. 242) might mean _____

   _____

8. **Canine** (p. 243) might mean _____

   _____

Let's see how you did. Check your answers, write the exact definitions,
and reread the sentence in *New Moon* where each word appears. Then
complete the drills on the next page.

1. **Dismissively** (p. 238) means *showing that something does not matter—dismissing it.*

2. **Hysteria** (p. 238) means *panic* or *intense emotion.* This reminds me of the great SAT and ACT word *histrionic* (dramatic), which was listed as a synonym for *melodramatic* in Group 7. You can see how they are related. *Panic* and *intense emotion* are very *dramatic.*

3. **Conspiratorially** (p. 239) means *plotting together.* Synonyms for *conspire:* collude, machinate, subterfuge.

4. **Blithely** (p. 240) means *with insensitive cheerfulness.* You have lots of clues for the meaning of this word. A few sentences before, Laurent "smiled," and soon after he "chuckled." He's downright "**cheerful**," and yet he's planning on having Bella for lunch—pretty **insensitive** if you ask me. He's making enemies though; who ever thought someone could irk Edward, Jacob, and Victoria all at one time!

5. **Serrated** (p. 240) means *jagged,* like a steak knife or a saw.

6. **Placate** (p. 241) means *soothe.* You saw this word as a synonym for *mollify* in Group 12. The other synonyms were *alleviate, ameliorate, assuage, conciliate, pacify,* and *palliate.* Another good one is *appease.*

7. **Incisors** (p. 242) means *sharp teeth.* You learned in Group 13 that *cis* implies *cutting,* and that is exactly what in**cis**ors are for.

8. **Canine** (p. 243) means *dog-like.* Let's look at a few other fancy dog terms: *vulpine* means *fox-like,* and *lupine* means *wolf-like.* Did you catch that one while you read the *Harry Potter* books? Yep, Professor **Lupin** is a **werewolf.** Like I said, J. K. Rowling and Stephenie Meyer have your back.

Synonyms: Select the word or phrase whose meaning is closest to the word in capital letters.

1. HYSTERIA
   A. compunction
   B. panic
   C. contrition
   D. repentance
   E. scruples

2. BLITHE
   A. cheerful
   B. canine
   C. vulpine
   D. lupine
   E. jagged

3. PLACATE
   A. dismiss
   B. conspire
   C. stymie
   D. foil
   E. appease

4. LUPINE
   A. cat-like
   B. cow-like
   C. wolf-like
   D. Edward-like
   E. Alice-like

Analogies: Select the answer choice that best completes the meaning of the sentence.

5. Hysteria is to composure as
   A. madness is to parched
   B. panic is to aplomb
   C. capitulation is to sangfroid
   D. aberrant is to equanimity
   E. petulance is to arid

6. Incisor is to tooth as
   A. dismissive is to conspirator
   B. serrated is to knife
   C. coven is to chasm
   D. solitary is to alone
   E. perforation is to hole

Sentence Completions: Choose the word or words that, when inserted in the sentence, <u>best</u> fits the meaning of the sentence as a whole.

7. Marvin had hoped to _____ Millie with his actions, but had no _____ effect at all.
   A. dismiss .. euphoric
   B. defile .. abrupt
   C. mutate .. foiling
   D. placate .. pacifying
   E. thwart .. dire

8. Peyton winked _____ at Lucas so he would understand the covert plan.
   A. conspiratorially
   B. blithely
   C. dismissively
   D. infectiously
   E. nebulously

1. **B.** *Hysteria* means *panic* or *intense emotion. Compunction, contrition, repentance,* and *scruples* mean *regret.*
2. **A.** *Blithe* means *insensitively cheerful,* so choice A is best. *Canine* means *dog-like, vulpine* means *fox-like,* and *lupine* means *Professor Lupin-like.*
3. **E.** *Placate* and *appease* both mean *soothe. Conspire* means *plot together. Stymie* and *foil* both mean *prevent.*
4. **C.** *Lupine* means *wolf-like.* It's a good thing I didn't have *Jacob-like* as an answer.
5. **B.** "Hysteria is the opposite of composure."
    - A. Madness is the opposite of parched (very dry) . . . no.
    - (B.) Panic is the opposite of aplomb (calmness) . . . yes.
    - C. Capitulation (surrender) is the opposite of sangfroid (calmness) . . . no.
    - D. Aberrant (abnormal) is the opposite of equanimity (calmness) . . . no.
    - E. Petulance (irritability) is the opposite of arid (very dry) . . . no.
6. **B.** "Incisor is a type of tooth."
    - A. Dismissive (dismissing) is a type of conspirator (plotter) . . . no. If an answer does not make sense to you, it's probably wrong. Never choose an answer **just** because it does not make sense. Trust yourself; if a choice seems confusing, then it's probably wrong.
    - (B.) Serrated (jagged) is a type of knife . . . yes, a steak knife is serrated.
    - C. Coven (vampire or witch group) is a type of chasm (deep pit) . . . no.
    - D. Solitary (alone) is a type of alone . . . no, they are synonyms, not "_____ is a type of _____."
    - E. Perforation (hole) is a type of hole . . . no, they are synonyms.
    If you find several choices that work, make your sentence more specific. "Incisor is a tooth" works for three choices, whereas the more specific "Incisor is a type of tooth" only works for choice B. This is a common analogy relationship: "_____ is a type of _____."
7. **D.** "Marvin had hoped to *????* Millie with his actions, but had no *????* effect at all."
    About once per test, the SAT has a sentence completion in which there is no evidence for what words you need for the blanks. In this case, decide if the words should have similar or opposite meanings. In this question, "Marvin had hoped to _____," "but had no _____ effect" so the words must be related. Use the process of elimination to look for the pair of similar words that fit best into the sentence. The words in choice D mean *soothe* and fit perfectly into the blanks.
8. **A.** "Peyton winked *plottingly* at Lucas so he would understand the covert plan."
    Conspiratorially means *plottingly.*

Group 22
Malicious Desire

Find each of the following words on the *New Moon* page number provided. Based on the way each word is used in the book, guess at its definition.

1. **Mammoth** (p. 243) might mean _____
   _____

2. **Stymie** (p. 249) might mean _____
   _____

3. **Foremost** (p. 252) might mean _____
   _____

4. **Secluded** (p. 255) might mean _____
   _____

5. **Brooding** (p. 259) might mean _____
   _____

6. **Prolonged** (p. 261) might mean _____
   _____

7. **Bile** (p. 263) might mean _____
   _____

8. **Malicious** (p. 263) might mean _____
   _____

Let's see how you did. Check your answers, write the exact definitions, and reread the sentence in *New Moon* where each word appears. Then complete the drills on the next page.

1. **Mammoth** (p. 243) means *huge*. On pages 242 and 243, Bella calls the wolf "huge," "enormous," "gigantic," "so *big*," and "monstrous in size," so you can definitely get this word's meaning from the context. Stephenie Meyer has already given you a bunch of the synonyms; three more good ones are *colossal, gargantuan,* and *immense*.

2. **Stymie** (p. 249) means *block* or *defeat* and was a synonym for *foil* in Group 18. The other synonym was *thwart*. I've seen these words tested many times on the SAT and ACT.

3. **Foremost** (p. 252) means *leading*, as in "first and foremost." This is a great word to break apart. *Fore-* means *in front,* so *foremost* means *most in front—leading*. Dr. Montgomery used this word when she was being sassed by Dr. Karev on *Grey's Anatomy*, "Dr. Karev, I may be a board-certified OB/GYN, but I also have fellowships in maternal-fetal medicine and medical genetics *and* am one of the **foremost** neonatal surgeons in this country. When you can top that, you can mouth off." (ABC, *Grey's Anatomy*, "Blues for Sister Someone," 2005)

4. **Secluded** (p. 255) means *out of the way* or *sheltered*.

5. **Brooding** (p. 259) means *preoccupied with unhappy thoughts*.

6. **Prolonged** (p. 261) means *unusually long*. Synonym: protracted.

7. **Bile** (p. 263) means *anger*. It actually relates to the bitter greenish-brown acid, called bile, that helps digestion. What's the connection? According to ancient Greek medicine too much bile causes **anger,** and that's where the meaning for *bile* comes from! Synonym: vitriol.

8. **Malicious** (p. 263) means *very hostile* or *wanting to harm* and was a synonym for *malevolent* in Group 19. Like *malevolent,* this word even sounds harmful, like the word *vicious*. Synonyms: abominable, baleful, execrable, loathsome, maleficent, malevolent, odious, rancorous, venomous.

Drills

Synonyms: Select the word or phrase whose meaning is closest to the word in capital letters.

1. MAMMOTH
   A. immense
   B. foremost
   C. secluded
   D. brooding
   E. maleficent

2. STYMIE
   A. prolong
   B. protract
   C. brood
   D. thwart
   E. placate

3. PROLONGED
   A. protracted
   B. alleviate
   C. ameliorate
   D. assuage
   E. conciliate

4. MALICIOUS
   A. dismissive
   B. histrionic
   C. blithe
   D. lupine
   E. malevolent

Analogies: Select the answer choice that best completes the meaning of the sentence.

5. Malicious is to harm as
   A. gigantic is to size
   B. secluded is to shelter
   C. foiled is to bile
   D. pacifying is to calm
   E. elated is to capitulation

6. Microscopic is to colossal as
   A. foremost is to first
   B. stymie is to assist
   C. brooding is to prolonged
   D. placated is to palliated
   E. incisor is to serrated

Sentence Completions: Choose the word that, when inserted in the sentence, best fits the meaning of the sentence as a whole.

7. Simone felt her bile stir as she realized that Alvin's callous actions would _____ her attempts to finish her project on time.
   A. brood
   B. seclude
   C. stymie
   D. blithe
   E. placate

8. Fans feel that Chester French's new keyboard player has immense talent and will be one of the _____ keyboard players in the world.
   A. foremost
   B. first
   C. secluded
   D. vulpine
   E. abrupt

1. **A.** *Mammoth* and *immense* mean *huge. Foremost* means *leading, secluded* means *sheltered, brooding* means *preoccupied with unhappy thoughts,* and *maleficent* means *causing harm.*

2. **D.** *Stymie* and *thwart* mean *prevent. Prolong* and *protract* mean *make longer,* which could happen from being prevented, but is not the definition of *stymie. Brood* means *be preoccupied with unhappy thoughts,* and *placate* means *soothe.*

3. **A.** *Prolonged* and *protracted* mean *very long. Alleviate, ameliorate, assuage,* and *conciliate* mean *soothe.*

4. **E.** *Malicious* and *malevolent* mean *harmful. Dismissive* means *considering something unimportant, histrionic* means *dramatic, blithe* means *insensitively cheerful,* and *lupine* means *wolf-like.*

5. **D.** "Malicious means causing harm."
   A . Gigantic means causing size . . . no, *gigantic* means *huge size.*
   B . Secluded means causing shelter . . . no, *secluded* means *sheltered.*
   C . Foiled means causing bile (anger) . . . no, *foiling* means *defeating.*
   (D.) Pacifying means causing calm . . . yes!
   E . Elated means causing capitulation (surrender) . . . no, *elated* means *joyful.*

6. **B.** "Microscopic is the opposite of colossal."
   A . Foremost (leading) is the opposite of first . . . no.
   (B.) Stymie (prevent) is the opposite of assist . . . yes.
   C . Brooding (preoccupied with unhappy thoughts) is the opposite of prolonged (very long) . . . no.
   D . Placated is the opposite of palliated . . . no, they both mean *soothed.*
   E . Incisor (sharp tooth) is the opposite of serrated (jagged) . . . no.

7. **C.** "Simone felt her bile stir as she realized that Alvin's callous actions would *effect/prevent* her attempts to finish her project on time."

   Use the process of elimination. *Stymie* means *block* and fits best. Watch out for choice A. Simone might *brood* (be preoccupied with unhappy thoughts) about it, but *brood* does not fit in the blank.

8. **A.** "Fans feel that Chester French's new keyboard player has immense talent and will be one of the *most talented* keyboard players in the world."

   Look for evidence, and when possible, use a word directly from the sentence to fill the blank. Then try each of the answer choices. *Foremost* means *leading* and fits best.

Taboo Dreams

Find each of the following words on the *New Moon* page number provided. Based on the way each word is used in the book, guess at its definition.

1. **Reeling** (p. 263) might mean _____

   _____

2. **Taboo** (p. 263) might mean _____

   _____

3. **Unperturbed** (p. 264) might mean _____

   _____

4. **Overt** (p. 265) might mean _____

   _____

5. **Brittle** (p. 266) might mean _____

   _____

6. **Livid** (p. 269) might mean _____

   _____

7. **Goaded** (p. 269) might mean _____

   _____

8. **Semblance** (p. 271) might mean _____

   _____

Let's see how you did. Check your answers, write the exact definitions, and reread the sentence in *New Moon* where each word appears. Then complete the drills on the next page.

1. **Reeling** (p. 263) means *staggering* or *bewildered,* usually from a setback.

2. **Taboo** (p. 263) means *forbidden.* Synonyms: illicit, interdicted, prohibited, proscribed. *New Moon* Quiz 3: Bella is referring to her fantasy of being a vampire. Why is that fantasy **taboo** for her right now? (Discuss with your friends.)

3. **Unperturbed** (p. 264) means *unconcerned.* That makes sense since *un-* means *not* and *perturbed* means *concerned.* You must be wondering what's up with Sam at this point. Good guy . . . or *imperious* (bossy) gang leader who's stolen Bella's best friend?

4. **Overt** (p. 265) means *obvious.* Synonyms: blatant, evident, manifest, patent. The words *furtive* and *surreptitious* from Groups 5 and 10 mean *secret* and are opposites (antonyms) of *overt.*

5. **Brittle** (p. 266) means *fragile* or *breakable,* like peanut **brittle,** a delicious peanut candy that you eat by **breaking** off pieces. "Mmmm, peanut brittle."

6. **Livid** (p. 269) means *furious* and was a synonym for *irate* in Group 13. Again, the context defines the word: "Jacob was **fuming** in front of me, quivering with **anger.**" Synonyms: incensed, infuriated, irate.

7. **Goaded** (p. 269) means *urged* and was a synonym for *prodded* in Group 10 and *coaxed* in Group 17. The other great SAT and ACT synonyms were *cajoled, enjoined, entreated, exhorted, implored* (begged), *incited,* and *spurred.*

8. **Semblance** (p. 271) means *appearance.* Remember to watch for connections to other languages. For example, in French *sembler* means *to appear.* Synonyms: facade, guise, pretense.

Synonyms: Select the word or phrase whose meaning is closest to the word in capital letters.

1. REELING
   A. overt
   B. blatant
   C. evident
   D. manifest
   E. stumbling

2. OVERT
   A. patent
   B. taboo
   C. illicit
   D. interdicted
   E. proscribed

3. BRITTLE
   A. livid
   B. fragile
   C. goading
   D. entreating
   E. spurring

4. LIVID
   A. irate
   B. gargantuan
   C. malicious
   D. malevolent
   E. solicitous

Analogies: Select the answer choice that best completes the meaning of the sentence.

5. Goad is to repress as
   A. coax is to entreat
   B. prod is to stifle
   C. enjoin is to exhort
   D. cajole is to incite
   E. implore is to spur

6. Livid is to angry as
   A. unperturbed is to concerned
   B. taboo is to appeased
   C. colossal is to big
   D. sallow is to tanned
   E. brooding is to happy

Sentence Completions: Choose the word that, when inserted in the sentence, best fits the meaning of the sentence as a whole.

7. Hoping to keep some semblance of her brittle ego intact, Jessica avoided Mike for several days and pretended to be _____ by their breakup.
   A. reeling
   B. stymied
   C. secluded
   D. unperturbed
   E. prolonged

8. Charlie knew that certain names were _____, and never to be uttered.
   A. taboo
   B. evident
   C. patent
   D. malicious
   E. secluded

1. **E.** *Reeling* means *stumbling from a setback;* Bella reels a lot. *Overt, blatant, evident,* and *manifest* mean *obvious.*

2. **A.** *Overt* and *patent* mean *obvious. Taboo, illicit, interdicted,* and *proscribed* mean *forbidden.*

3. **B.** *Brittle* means *fragile. Livid* means *very angry. Goading, entreating,* and *spurring* mean *urging.*

4. **A.** *Livid* and *irate* mean *very angry. Gargantuan* means *huge. Malicious* and *malevolent* mean *harmful,* and *solicitous* means *concerned.*

5. **B.** "Goad (urge) is the opposite of repress."
    A. Coax (urge) is the opposite of entreat (urge) . . . no.
    B. Prod (urge) is the opposite of stifle . . . yes!
    C. Enjoin (urge) is the opposite of exhort (urge) . . . no.
    D. Cajole (urge) is the opposite of incite (urge) . . . no.
    E. Implore (urge) is the opposite of spur (urge) . . . no.

6. **C.** "Livid means very angry."
    A. Unperturbed means very concerned . . . no, *unperturbed* means **not** *concerned.*
    B. Taboo (forbidden) means very appeased (soothed) . . . no.
    C. Colossal means very big . . . yes!
    D. Sallow means very tanned . . . no, *sallow* means *pale.*
    E. Brooding (preoccupied with unhappy thoughts) means very happy . . . no.

7. **D.** "Hoping to keep some semblance of her brittle ego intact, Jessica avoided Mike for several days and pretended to be _not bothered_ by their breakup."

    Unperturbed means *not bothered.* This sentence hints at the answer, but does not define it. Look for evidence, but when you are not sure what word you'd like to see for the blank, decide if the word should be positive or negative, and then use the process of elimination. Especially in this case, it's critical to eliminate choices **only** when you are absolutely positive that they don't fit. Then choose the best of the remaining choices.

8. **A.** "Charlie knew that certain names were _never to be uttered,_ and never to be uttered."

    Think of a word you'd like to see, taking a word or words right from the sentence when possible and then use the process of elimination. *Taboo* means *forbidden.*

Group 24

Jake's New Agility?

Find each of the following words on the *New Moon* page number provided. Based on the way each word is used in the book, guess at its definition.

1. **Unrequited** (p. 276) might mean _____

   _____

2. **Grating** (p. 279) might mean _____

   _____

3. **Maim** (p. 280) might mean _____

   _____

4. **Agilely** (p. 280) might mean _____

   _____

5. **Smirking** (p. 280) might mean _____

   _____

6. **En masse** (p. 281) might mean _____

   _____

7. **Ineptly** (p. 285) might mean _____

   _____

8. **Prelude** (p. 286) might mean _____

   _____

Let's see how you did. Check your answers, write the exact definitions,
and reread the sentence in *New Moon* where each word appears. Then
complete the drills on the next page.

1. **Unrequited** (p. 276) means *not returned.* Synonym: unreciprocated.
   Unrequited crushes are big in these books—Mike, Bella, Jacob—
   but hey, that's high school.

2. **Grating** (p. 279) means *harsh.* Synonym: strident.

3. **Maim** (p. 280) means *permanently injure.* In Group 4, you learned
   that *mayhem* (violent disorder) comes from the word *maim.*

4. **Agilely** (p. 280) means *gracefully.* Synonyms for *agile:* adept, adroit,
   deft, dexterous, lithe, nimble, supple.

5. **Smirking** (p. 280) means *smiling in an annoying way.* A few lines
   before "... a wide grin spread slowly across Jacob's face ... ," and
   the smile itself might not be annoying, but Bella finds it annoying
   that Jacob rejected her and is now smiling "as if none of that had
   passed."

6. **En masse** (p. 281) means *grouped together.* This expression literally
   translates from French as "in a mass."

7. **Ineptly** (p. 285) means *without skill.* This is a cool word to break
   apart. *In-* means *not* or *without,* and *-ept* refers to *apt,* meaning *able,*
   like in the word *adept* (able, skilled).

8. **Prelude** (p. 286) means *introduction.* Remember from Group 8 that
   pre- means *before.* Synonyms: commencement, overture, precursor.

Synonyms: Select the word or phrase whose meaning is closest to the word in capital letters.

1. UNREQUITED
   A. unperturbed
   B. patent
   C. infuriated
   D. unreciprocated
   E. ecstatic

2. AGILE
   A. reeling
   B. maimed
   C. nimble
   D. baleful
   E. abominable

3. INEPT
   A. grating
   B. strident
   C. smirking
   D. en masse
   E. clumsy

4. PRELUDE
   A. overture
   B. taboo
   C. semblance
   D. hysteria
   E. bile

Analogies: Select the answer choice that best completes the meaning of the sentence.

5. Smirking is to smiling as
   A. grimacing is to albino
   B. monotone is to morose
   C. nefarious is to antisocial
   D. blithe is to happiness
   E. tranquil is to severed

6. En masse is to solitarily as
   A. glacial is to interspersed
   B. perquisite is to rectifiable
   C. aberrant is to ordinary
   D. surreptitious is to poignant
   E. sinister is to tolerant

Sentence Completions: Choose the word that, when inserted in the sentence, <u>best</u> fits the meaning of the sentence as a whole.

7. The _____ ceremonies signal the beginning of a new phase for graduating students.
   A. commencement
   B. unrequited
   C. grating
   D. strident
   E. adept

8. Michael Jordan displayed such _____ and graceful movements that it seemed he was flying through the air.
   A. heady
   B. adroit
   C. impulsive
   D. ironic
   E. contorted

1. **D.** *Unrequited* and *unreciprocated* mean *not returned.* *Unperturbed* means *unconcerned,* *patent* means *obvious,* *infuriated* means *very angry,* and *ecstatic* means *very excited.*

2. **C.** *Agile* and *nimble* mean *graceful.* *Maimed* means *permanently injured,* *reeling* means *staggering,* and *baleful* and *abominable* mean *wicked.*

3. **E.** *Inept* means *unskilled* or *clumsy.* *Grating* and *strident* mean *harsh,* *smirking* means *smiling annoyingly,* and *en masse* means *grouped together.*

4. **A.** *Prelude* and *overture* both mean *introduction.* *Taboo* means *forbidden,* *semblance* means *appearance,* *hysteria* means *intense emotions,* and *bile* means *anger.*

5. **D.** "Smirking means annoying smiling."
   - A . Grimacing (frowning) means annoying albino . . . no, that makes no sense.
   - B . Monotone (dull) means annoying morose (sad) . . . no, that makes no sense.
   - C . Nefarious (wicked) means annoying antisocial (alone) . . . no, that makes no sense.
   - (D.) Blithe (insensitive cheerfulness) means annoying happiness . . . yes!
   - E . Tranquil (calm) means annoying severed (cut) . . . no, that makes no sense.

6. **C.** "En masse (together) is the opposite of solitarily (alone)."
   Look at all these great words that you've learned!
   - A . Glacial (icy) is the opposite of interspersed (scattered) . . . no.
   - B . Perquisite (benefit) is the opposite of rectifiable (fixable) . . . no.
   - (C.) Aberrant (abnormal) is the opposite of ordinary . . . yes!
   - D. Surreptitious (secretive) is the opposite of poignant (touching) . . . no.
   - E . Sinister (wicked) is the opposite of tolerant (lenient) . . . no.

7. **A.** "The _beginning_ ceremonies signal the beginning of a new phase for graduating students."
   Commencement means *beginning.*

8. **B.** "Michael Jordan displayed such _graceful_ and graceful movements that it seemed he was flying through the air."
   Adroit means *graceful.* Several answers might seem to work, but the sentence provides most direct and specific evidence for choice B—Jordan had "graceful," not *contorted,* movements and "flew through the air."

Group 25

Mythical Monsters

Find each of the following words on the *New Moon* page number provided. Based on the way each word is used in the book, guess at its definition.

1. **Jade** (p. 290) might mean _____

   _____

2. **Stock** (p. 293) might mean _____

   _____

3. **Mythical** (p. 294) might mean _____

   _____

4. **Absolute** (p. 294) might mean _____

   _____

5. **Carcasses** (p. 296) might mean _____

   _____

6. **Octaves** (p. 296) might mean _____

   _____

7. **Reverberated** (p. 301) might mean _____

   _____

8. **Stoic** (p. 301) might mean _____

   _____

Let's see how you did. Check your answers, write the exact definitions, and reread the sentence in *New Moon* where each word appears. Then complete the drills on the next page.

1. **Jade** (p. 290) means *green with a bluish tint.* The word comes from the name of the mineral, jade, which can actually have several different shades. Interestingly, in Chinese culture, giving jade or jade-colored objects is an expression of love. Is Stephenie Meyer telling us something about Bella and Jacob?

2. **Stock** (p. 293) in this case means *belief.* It can also mean *products carried by a store* (as in "Do you have the *New Moon* DVD in **stock** yet?") or *ownership of a business* (as in "Cool, I got five shares of Toyota Corporation **stock** for my birthday!"). This is another great example of a word with several meanings that the SAT, ACT, GED, or SSAT might use in a reading comprehension question. The question might offer *products* and *ownership* as answers, and you will have to decide how it is used in the context of the passage. On these questions, always reread a few sentences before and a few sentences after the word.

3. **Mythical** (p. 294) means *legendary—of myths.*

4. **Absolute** (p. 294) means *total.* Synonyms: consummate, unconditional, unequivocal, unmitigated, unqualified. You saw this word in Group 6 as *absolutely,* but it and its synonyms show up so often on tests, that I included it again here.

5. **Carcasses** (p. 296) means *dead **animal** bodies.* Dead **human** bodies are called *corpses.* I'm not sure what dead **vampire** bodies are called, but they are pretty rare anyway.

6. **Octaves** (p. 296) means *a series of eight notes.* The prefix *oct-* means *eight,* as in *octagon* (a shape with eight sides), *octet* (a group of eight musicians or instruments, or an eight-line poem), and *octopus* (a creature with eight legs).

7. **Reverberated** (p. 301) means *echoed.*

8. **Stoic** (p. 301), like *impassive* from Group 7, means *not showing emotion.*

Synonyms: Select the word or phrase whose meaning is closest to the word in capital letters.

1. MYTHICAL
   A. legendary
   B. jade
   C. unequivocal
   D. unmitigated
   E. unqualified

2. ABSOLUTE
   A. octopus
   B. supple
   C. unrequited
   D. grating
   E. consummate

3. REVERBERATE
   A. stock
   B. smirk
   C. echo
   D. maim
   E. goad

4. STOIC
   A. inept
   B. en masse
   C. deft
   D. impassive
   E. strident

Analogies: Select the answer choice that best completes the meaning of the sentence.

5. Carcass is to corpse as
   A. animal is to human
   B. jade is to color
   C. stock is to belief
   D. unrequited is to crush
   E. overture is to finale

6. Octopus is to legs as
   A. octave is to music
   B. octagon is to shapes
   C. October is to months
   D. octahedron is to hedrons
   E. octet is to lines

Sentence Completions: Choose the word that, when inserted in the sentence, best fits the meaning of the sentence as a whole.

7. Francis did not take much stock in the rumors and _____ about the jade pendant's magical powers.
   A. carcasses
   B. octaves
   C. precursors
   D. compunctions
   E. myths

8. The mythical beast Grendel attacked Beowulf's army and dominated the battle, leaving many _____ behind.
   A. myths
   B. corpses
   C. reverberations
   D. taboos
   E. semblances

1. **A.** *Mythical* means *legendary. Jade* means *bluish-green,* and *unequivocal, unmitigated,* and *unqualified* mean *complete.*

2. **E.** *Absolute* and *consummate* mean *total.* Use the process of elimination; only choice E is close. *Supple* means *graceful* or *flexible. Unrequited* means *unreturned,* and *grating* means *harsh.*

3. **C.** *Reverberate* means *echo. Stock* means *belief, products,* or *ownership. Smirk* means *smile annoyingly, maim* means *permanently injure,* and *goad* means *urge.*

4. **D.** *Stoic* and *impassive* mean *not showing feelings*—not letting someone else "**pass in**to their feelings." In fact, *impassive* always makes me think of *Monty Python and the Holy Grail* and the scene where the Black Knight says, "None shall pass." (Twentieth Century Fox, 1975)

5. **A.** "Carcass is to corpse."

   If you can't make a relationship between the words in the question that makes sense for the answer choices, try using the setup from Group 16, where the words in the question relate not to each other, but to the words in the answer choices. Choice A is best since **carcass** is a *dead **animal** body,* and **corpse** is a *dead **human** body.*

6. **E.** "An octopus has eight legs."
   - A. An octave has eight music . . . no.
   - B. An octagon has eight shapes . . . no, an *octagon* is *a shape with eight sides.*
   - C. October has eight months . . . no, and why does October have *oct-* when it's the tenth month? When it was named, back in Roman times, it was the eighth month!
   - D. An octahedron has eight hedrons . . . no, in fact *hedron* is not even a real word!
   - E. An octet has eight lines . . . yes, it is *an eight-line poem.*

7. **E.** "Francis did not take much stock in the rumors and <u>rumors</u> about the jade pendant's magical powers."

   Myths means *legends* and is the best answer.

8. **B.** "The mythical beast Grendel attacked Beowulf's army and dominated the battle, leaving many <u>????</u> behind."

   Corpses means *dead bodies.* Use evidence in the sentence to choose your answer. The beast attacked and dominated, so *corpses* makes sense. The creature may have left myths or taboos behind, but the evidence in the sentence most directly supports *corpses.*

Quiz 5

I. Let's review some of the words that you've seen in Groups 21–25. Match each of the following words to the correct definition or synonym on the right. Then check the solutions on page 172.

1. Hysteria	A. Insensitively cheerful
2. Blithe	B. Gargantuan
3. Placate	C. Patent
4. Mammoth	D. Appease
5. Stymie	E. Panic
6. Malicious	F. Foil
7. Taboo	G. Adroit
8. Overt	H. Maleficent
9. Goad	I. Echo
10. Unrequited	J. Illicit
11. Agile	K. Impassive
12. Prelude	L. Coax
13. Absolute	M. Unreciprocated
14. Reverberate	N. Unconditional
15. Stoic	O. Overture

II. Let's review several of the word parts that you've seen in Groups 21–25. Match each of the following word parts to the correct definition or synonym on the right. Then check the solutions on page 172.

16. Cis-	A. In front
17. Oct-	B. Before
18. Fore-	C. Not
19. Pre-	D. Cut
20. Un-	E. Not
21. In-	F. Eight

Group 26

Transformation

Find each of the following words on the *New Moon* page number provided.
Based on the way each word is used in the book, guess at its definition.

1. **Castanets** (p. 305) might mean _____

   _____

2. **Morph** (p. 308) might mean _____

   _____

3. **Solemnly** (p. 308) might mean _____

   _____

4. **Cowered** (p. 323) might mean _____

   _____

5. **Synchronization** (p. 323) might mean _____

   _____

6. **Coalescing** (p. 325) might mean _____

   _____

7. **Transformation** (p. 325) might mean _____

   _____

8. **Rapt** (p. 326) might mean _____

   _____

Let's see how you did. Check your answers, write the exact definitions, and reread the sentence in *New Moon* where each word appears. Then complete the drills on the next page.

Definitions

1. **Castanets** (p. 305) are *small, shell-shaped percussion instruments.*

2. **Morph** (p. 308) means *change.* It is actually short for the word *metamorphosis,* which also means *change,* as in the *metamorphosis* of a caterpillar into a butterfly, or the *metamorphosis* of a human into a werewolf. The word part *morph-* actually means *form* or *shape,* while *meta-* is the part that means *change.*

3. **Solemnly** (p. 308) means *seriously.* Synonyms: earnestly, gravely, sincerely, soberly, somberly.

4. **Cowered** (p. 323) means *hid fearfully,* and looks a lot like the word *coward* (a fearful person).

5. **Synchronization** (p. 323) means *coordination* or *harmonizing,* like Justin Timberlake, JC Chasez, Joey Fatone, and the other "boys" of 'N Sync do when they sing.

6. **Coalescing** (p. 325) means *coming together.* That makes sense since the prefix *co-* means *together.* Synonyms: amalgamating, converging, fusing, homogenizing. *Homogenizing* is a cool word to break apart. *Homo-* means *same,* so *homogenizing* means *making all of something uniform* (the same).

7. **Transformation** (p. 325) is a synonym for *metamorphosis* and means *change.* *Trans-* means *across,* so a *transformation* is a *change across forms.* *Trans-* is one of the most useful prefixes for the SAT, ACT, GED, and SSAT. It helps you with great words such as *transgress* (go across boundaries—cheat); *transcribe* (*-scribe* means *write,* so *transcribe* means *write from one form to another*); and *transcontinental* (across a continent).

8. **Rapt** (p. 326) means *fascinated.* Synonyms: captivated, enthralled, mesmerized, riveted.

Synonyms: Select the word or phrase whose meaning is closest to the word in capital letters.

1. MORPH
   A. change
   B. cower
   C. enthrall
   D. mesmerize
   E. captivate

2. SOLEMN
   A. riveted
   B. rapt
   C. mythical
   D. somber
   E. stoic

3. SYNCHRONIZE
   A. reverberate
   B. harmonize
   C. requite
   D. reciprocate
   E. cajole

4. COALESCE
   A. mollify
   B. thwart
   C. fuse
   D. excise
   E. infiltrate

Analogies: Select the answer choice that best completes the meaning of the sentence.

5. Castanets is to percussion as
   A. carcass is to animal
   B. gemstone is to jade
   C. octave is to music
   D. abyss is to void
   E. flute is to woodwind

6. Coalesce is to come together as
   A. amalgamate is to break apart
   B. fuse is to cower
   C. homogenize is to make uniform
   D. synchronize is to perforate
   E. harmonize is to cede

Sentence Completions: Choose the word or words that, when inserted in the sentence, <u>best</u> fits the meaning of the sentence as a whole.

7. Jayley cowered beside her parents as she solemnly swore to the headmaster that she had not _____ nor broken any aspects of the school's honor code.
   A. transcribed
   B. transformed
   C. paid homage
   D. transgressed
   E. rapt

8. With _____ and undivided attention, the children waited for the magician to pull the rabbit from his hat.
   A. coalescing
   B. rapt
   C. stoic
   D. unrequited
   E. agile

1. **A.** *Morph* means *change*. *Cower* means *hide in fear*. *Enthrall*, *mesmerize*, and *captivate* mean *fascinate*.

2. **D.** *Solemn* and *somber* mean *serious*. *Riveted* and *rapt* mean *fascinated*. *Mythical* means *legendary*, and *stoic* means *not showing emotion*.

3. **B.** *Synchronize* means *harmonize*. *Reverberate* means *echo*. *Requite* and *reciprocate* mean *return* or *pay back*, and *cajole* means *urge*.

4. **C.** *Coalesce* means *bring together*. *Fuse*, which means *join*, is the closest answer. As always, use the process of elimination to find the closest answer—cross off answers that you are **sure** don't work and choose the best of what's left. *Mollify* means *soothe*, *thwart* means *prevent*, *excise* means *remove*, and *infiltrate* means *enter*.

5. **E.** "Castanets are a type of percussion."
   A. A carcass is a type of animal . . . no, a *carcass* is a *dead animal*.
   B. A gemstone is a type of jade . . . no, that's backwards.
   C. An octave is a type of music . . . no, *octave* is a *musical term*.
   D. An abyss (bottomless pit) is a type of void (emptiness) . . . maybe, but it's a weak connection.
   (E.) A flute is a type of woodwind . . . yes, perfect, and much better than choice D!

6. **C.** "Coalesce means come together."
   A. Amalgamate (bring together) means break apart . . . no.
   B. Fuse (bring together) means cower (hide in fear) . . . no.
   (C.) Homogenize (make all the same) means make uniform . . . yes!
   D. Synchronize (coordinate or harmonize) means perforate (make holes) . . . no.
   E. Harmonize means cede (surrender) . . . no.

7. **D.** "Jayley cowered beside her parents as she solemnly swore to the headmaster that she had not *cheated* nor broken any aspects of the school's honor code."
   Transgressed means *cheated on a code or principle* and fits perfectly. Choice C, *paid homage* (honored) is about honor, but not about breaking it.

8. **B.** "With *undivided* and undivided attention, the children waited for the magician to pull the rabbit from his hat."
   Rapt, meaning *fascinated*, fits best. *Coalescing* (coming together) is similar to *undivided* but does not describe attention and does not fit with the rest of the sentence. *Stoic* (impassive), *unrequited* (not returned), and *agile* (graceful) do not fit the evidence of the sentence.

Tattered Remnants

Find each of the following words on the *New Moon* page number provided. Based on the way each word is used in the book, guess at its definition.

1. **Remnants** (p. 327) might mean _____

_____

2. **Injunction** (p. 329) might mean _____

_____

3. **Scrounge** (p. 329) might mean _____

_____

4. **Timidly** (p. 331) might mean _____

_____

5. **Chastised** (p. 332) might mean _____

_____

6. **Banter** (p. 333) might mean _____

_____

7. **Humongous** (p. 333) might mean _____

_____

8. **Intrusive** (p. 333) might mean _____

_____

Let's see how you did. Check your answers, write the exact definitions, and reread the sentence in *New Moon* where each word appears. Then complete the drills on the next page.

1. **Remnants** (p. 327) means *leftovers,* the part remaining.

2. **Injunction** (p. 329) means *formal order.* You can see that in the context. Embry asked Bella how Jacob had gotten around the *injunction,* and when she didn't understand, Embry repeated, "Er, the **order.**" Embry defined it right there for you. *Injunction* is another synonym for *edict* from Group 18. The other synonyms were *decree, fiat, mandate,* and *proclamation.* Three more good ones are *dictum, directive,* and *writ.*

3. **Scrounge** (p. 329) means *dig.*

4. **Timidly** (p. 331) means *shyly* or *with fear.* Synonyms: apprehensively, diffidently, pusillanimously, timorously. SAT sentence-completion questions are arranged in order of difficulty, from easiest to hardest. The easier questions usually have easier words as answers, and the harder questions usually have harder words. *Pusillanimous* is a perfect example of a harder word. I've seen it as the answer to a "hard" question, but now you know it, so for you it'll be easy.

5. **Chastised** (p. 332) means *scolded.* Chastised was a synonym for *rebuked* in Group 13. The other synonyms were *admonished, censured, reprimanded, reproached,* and *reproved.* Remember that *admonished* and *reproached* are *less stern (more gentle) scolds.*

6. **Banter** (p. 333) means *joke back and forth.* Synonyms: badinage, raillery, repartee.

7. **Humongous** (p. 333) means *huge,* just like *colossal, enormous, gargantuan, gigantic, immense, mammoth,* and *monstrous* from Group 22. Here's a great way to remember the word *colossal* and a tough quiz even for you *Twilight* diehards: Which *New Moon* movie actor played the **huge** mutant **"Colossus"** in the films *X2* and *X-Men: The Last Stand?* See answers on page 172.

8. **Intrusive** (p. 333) means *invasive.*

Synonyms: Select the word or phrase whose meaning is closest to the word in capital letters.

1. REMNANTS
   - A. dictum
   - B. directive
   - C. writ
   - D. leftovers
   - E. mandate

2. INJUNCTION
   - A. fiat
   - B. repartee
   - C. raillery
   - D. badinage
   - E. banter

3. TIMID
   - A. gigantic
   - B. gargantuan
   - C. pusillanimous
   - D. colossal
   - E. immense

4. CHASTISE
   - A. scrounge
   - B. rebuke
   - C. morph
   - D. cower
   - E. synchronize

Analogies: Select the answer choice that best completes the meaning of the sentence.

5. Injunction is to compel as
   - A. castanets is to perturb
   - B. transformation is to goad
   - C. fusing is to implore
   - D. mandate is to require
   - E. homogenizing is to enjoin

6. Banter is to laugh as
   - A. scrounging is to intrude
   - B. courage is to timid
   - C. transformation is to capitulate
   - D. compunction is to regret
   - E. semblance is to livid

Sentence Completions: Choose the word that, when inserted in the sentence, <u>best</u> fits the meaning of the sentence as a whole.

7. Sienna _____ approached the principal, apprehensive about whether he would let her take the day off to attend the *New Moon* movie premier.
   - A. intrusively
   - B. stoically
   - C. timorously
   - D. ineptly
   - E. maliciously

8. The mayor believed that her _____ of the council's careless spending would end the wastefulness, and hoped that an injunction would not be necessary.
   - A. rebuke
   - B. scrounging
   - C. banter
   - D. coalescing
   - E. amalgamating

Solutions

1. **D.** *Remnants* means *leftovers. Dictum, directive, writ,* and *mandate* mean *formal order.*

2. **A.** *Injunction* and *fiat* mean *formal order. Repartee, raillery, badinage,* and *banter* mean *joking back and forth.*

3. **C.** *Timid* and *pusillanimous* mean *shy and fearful. Gigantic, gargantuan, colossal,* and *immense* mean *huge.*

4. **B.** *Chastise* and *rebuke* mean *scold. Scrounge* means *dig, morph* means *change, cower* means *hide in fear,* and *synchronize* means *coordinate.*

5. **D.** "An injunction (formal declaration) might compel someone to do something."
   A. Castanets (percussion instruments) might perturb (disturb) someone to do something . . . no, not unless she or he really hates castanets.
   B. A transformation (change) might goad (urge) someone to do something . . . no.
   C. Fusing (joining) might implore (urge) someone to do something . . . no.
   (D.) A mandate (formal declaration) might require someone to do something . . . yes!
   E. Homogenizing (making all the same) might enjoin (urge) someone to do something . . . no.

6. **D.** "Banter might make a person laugh."
   A. Scrounging (digging) might make a person intrude . . . no, not necessarily.
   B. Courage might make a person timid (shy) . . . no.
   C. Transformation (change) might make a person capitulate (surrender) . . . no.
   (D.) Compunction (morals, regrets) might make a person regret . . . yes!
   E. Semblance (appearance) might make a person livid (very angry) . . . no, not necessarily.

7. **C.** "Sienna *apprehensively* approached the principal, apprehensive about whether he would let her take the day off to attend the *New Moon* movie premier."
   Timorously means *apprehensively.* Sienna may have also been *intrusive* (invasive), *stoical* (impassive), *inept* (unskilled), or even *malicious* (hostile), but you have evidence only that she was apprehensive.

8. **A.** "The mayor believed that her *criticism* of the council's careless spending would end the wastefulness, and hoped that an injunction would not be necessary."
   Rebuke means *scolding* and fits best. That is certainly the best answer using the process of elimination. *Scrounging* means *digging, banter* means *jokes,* and *coalescing* and *amalgamating* mean *bringing together.*

Group 28

Avenging

Find each of the following words on the *New Moon* page number provided. Based on the way each word is used in the book, guess at its definition.

1. **Wretched** (p. 333) might mean _____
   _____

2. **Exultant** (p. 334) might mean _____
   _____

3. **Avenge** (p. 335) might mean _____
   _____

4. **Unabashed** (p. 336) might mean _____
   _____

5. **Intermittently** (p. 338) might mean _____
   _____

6. **Scant** (p. 339) might mean _____
   _____

7. **Sophomore** (p. 343) might mean _____
   _____

8. **Shrewdly** (p. 343) might mean _____
   _____

Let's see how you did. Check your answers, write the exact definitions, and reread the sentence in *New Moon* where each word appears. Then complete the drills on the next page.

1. **Wretched** (p. 333) means *miserable*. With Edward gone, there are a lot of words for *miserable* in *New Moon*. Synonyms: desolate, devastated, disconsolate.

2. **Exultant** (p. 334) is the opposite of *wretched*. It means *very excited* and was a synonym for *exuberant* in Group 15 and *elated* in Group 20. The other synonyms were *buoyant, ebullient, ecstatic, euphoric, jubilant,* and *rapturous.*

3. **Avenge** (p. 335) means *get revenge* and even sounds like *revenge*. When you find a word you don't know, feel it out. You might be surprised how often feeling it out gets you close to the real meaning!

4. **Unabashed** (p. 336) means *unashamed*. Guess what *abashed* means? Yep, since *un-* means *not, abashed* means *ashamed.*

5. **Intermittently** (p. 338) means *on and off* or *sporadically.*

6. **Scant** (p. 339) means *little*. The SAT, ACT, and SSAT love the synonyms *inadequate, meager, negligible,* and *paltry*. And a super-cool synonym that you'll only see on a "hard" question is *exiguous.*

7. **Sophomore** (p. 343) in this case means *a high school student in tenth grade*. You knew that, but I included this word so I could show you the great high-level SAT and ACT word *sophomoric,* which means *childish*. Sorry Jake, but I didn't invent it. I just wanted to mention it since it shows up so often on the tests.

8. **Shrewdly** (p. 343) means *wisely*. It usually implies some selfishness in the wisdom—do you think that Mike has some selfishness in pointing out Jacob's feelings to Bella? Synonyms: astutely, cannily, cunningly, perspicaciously, sagaciously.

Synonyms: Select the word or phrase whose meaning is closest to the word in capital letters.

1. WRETCHED
   A. disconsolate
   B. astute
   C. canny
   D. cunning
   E. perspicacious

2. EXULTANT
   A. timid
   B. diffident
   C. rapturous
   D. pusillanimous
   E. humongous

3. INTERMITTENT
   A. sophomoric
   B. sporadic
   C. sagacious
   D. negligible
   E. paltry

4. SCANT
   A. exiguous
   B. cowering
   C. captivated
   D. rapt
   E. consummate

Analogies: Select the answer choice that best completes the meaning of the sentence.

5. Desolate is to euphoric as
   A. wretched is to mammoth
   B. shrewd is to inept
   C. unabashed is to grave
   D. devastated is to solemn
   E. converging is to amalgamated

6. Victoria is to avenge as
   A. Edward is to chastise
   B. Sam is to coalesce
   C. Jacob is to protect
   D. Emily is to spur
   E. Lauren is to stymie

Sentence Completions: Choose the word that, when inserted in the sentence, best fits the meaning of the sentence as a whole.

7. People on the crowded bus were equally surprised by the couple's _____ display of affection and by their apparent lack of self-consciousness.
   A. shrewd
   B. sagacious
   C. unabashed
   D. meager
   E. blithe

8. Most tenth graders are not _____, in fact they usually exhibit a high level of sophistication and maturity.
   A. buoyant
   B. ebullient
   C. jubilant
   D. unremitting
   E. sophomoric

1. **A.** *Wretched* and *disconsolate* mean *miserable*. *Astute, canny, cunning,* and *perspicacious* mean *wise*.

2. **C.** *Exultant* and *rapturous* mean *very excited*. *Timid, diffident,* and *pusillanimous* mean *shy or fearful*. *Humongous* means *very large*.

3. **B.** *Intermittent* and *sporadic* mean *on and off*. *Sophomoric* means *childish* (sorry Jake), *sagacious* means *wise*, and *negligible* and *paltry* mean *little*.

4. **A.** *Scant* and *exiguous* mean *little*, as in "compared to Edward, Bella has **exiguous** resources to pay for college." Use *exiguous* in your SAT, ACT, GED, or SSAT essay and I guarantee that you'll gain a point! *Cowering* means *hiding fearfully*, *captivated* and *rapt* mean *enthralled*, and *consummate* means *complete*.

5. **B.** "Desolate (miserable) is the opposite of euphoric (very excited)."
   A. Wretched is the opposite of mammoth (huge) . . . no.
   (B.) Shrewd (wise) is the opposite of inept (unskilled) . . . maybe.
   C. Unabashed (unashamed) is the opposite of grave (serious) . . . no.
   D. Devastated is the opposite of solemn (serious) . . . no.
   E. Converging (coming together) is the opposite of amalgamated (came together) . . . no.
   Using the process of elimination, choice B is best.

6. **C.** "Victoria wants to avenge (get revenge for) James."
   A. Edward wants to chastise (scold) Bella . . . no, not necessarily.
   B. Sam wants to coalesce (bring together) Emily . . . no, that makes no sense.
   (C.) Jacob wants to protect Bella . . . yes!
   D. Emily wants to spur (urge) Sam . . . no, that makes no sense.
   E. Lauren wants to stymie (block) Ben . . . no.

7. **C.** "People on the crowded bus were equally surprised by the couple's *not self-conscious* display of affection and by their apparent lack of self-consciousness."
   Unabashed means *not self-conscious*. *Blithe*, from Group 21, means *insensitively cheerful*.

8. **E.** "Most tenth graders are not *immature*, in fact they usually exhibit a high level of sophistication and maturity."
   Sophomoric means *childish*. Several other answers sound decent when placed in the blank, but only *sophomoric* is supported by the evidence in the question—"in fact" tells you that the blank relates to the opposite of "sophistication and maturity."

Group 29

Velvet Intonation

Find each of the following words on the *New Moon* page number provided. Based on the way each word is used in the book, guess at its definition.

1. **Compelled** (p. 349) might mean _____

   _____

2. **Ascertain** (p. 350) might mean _____

   _____

3. **Sultry** (p. 353) might mean _____

   _____

4. **Unendurable** (p. 355) might mean _____

   _____

5. **Festering** (p. 356) might mean _____

   _____

6. **Eerie** (p. 356) might mean _____

   _____

7. **Eddies** (p. 358) might mean _____

   _____

8. **Intonation** (p. 358) might mean _____

   _____

Let's see how you did. Check your answers, write the exact definitions, and reread the sentence in *New Moon* where each word appears. Then complete the drills on the next page.

1. **Compelled** (p. 349) means *required,* like when Ron Burgundy says, "I don't normally do this, but I felt **compelled** to tell you something." You can only imagine what sort of shenanigans he's going to say next! (DreamWorks, *Anchorman: The Legend of Ron Burgundy,* 2004) You learned *compel* as the root word of *compulsion* (obsession) in Group 9.

2. **Ascertain** (p. 350) means *find out for sure.* It even sounds like "as certain," which is what it means—to confirm something **as certain.** Bella wants to confirm **as certain** that Jacob is okay. He is, after all, hunting a lethal, nefarious, and avenging vampire.

3. **Sultry** (p. 353) means *hot and humid.* You can get this from the context. There is a thick layer of clouds, so it's not sunny. And Bella says that it's warm, so since this is Forks, it's **warm** and **wet**—sultry.

4. **Unendurable** (p. 355) means *not endurable—unbearable.* Synonym: intolerable.

5. **Festering** (p. 356) means *getting much worse,* like a wound that gets infected.

6. **Eerie** (p. 356) means *spooky.* SAT, ACT, GED, and SSAT reading-comprehension passages always include a few questions about the tone of a passage. **Tone** is expressed through an author's choice of words and punctuation. You can see the *ominous* (threatening) tone of this page from words like "festering" and "eerie," as well as "revenge," "angrier," "shivered," and "trick." Something's up, that's for sure!

7. **Eddies** (p. 358) means *swirls of water or wind.*

8. **Intonation** (p. 358) means *pitch.* Synonyms: cadence, inflection, timber.

Synonyms: Select the word or phrase whose meaning is closest to the word in capital letters.

1. COMPEL
   A. require
   B. ascertain
   C. endure
   D. fester
   E. avenge

2. SULTRY
   A. eerie
   B. disconsolate
   C. buoyant
   D. sagacious
   E. humid

3. UNENDURABLE
   A. desolate
   B. intolerable
   C. ebullient
   D. intermittent
   E. meager

4. INTONATION
   A. injunction
   B. dictum
   C. inflection
   D. writ
   E. metamorphosis

Analogies: Select the answer choice that best completes the meaning of the sentence.

5. Fester is to worse as
   A. ascertain is to indifferent
   B. morph is to amalgamated
   C. convalesce is to better
   D. homogenize is to varied
   E. reel is to brittle

6. Sultry is to arid as
   A. eddies is to swirls
   B. cadence is to timber
   C. prolonged is to protracted
   D. secluded is to communal
   E. stymie is to thwart

Sentence Completions: Choose the word that, when inserted in the sentence, <u>best</u> fits the meaning of the sentence as a whole.

7. Even though Kirsten is already a successful professional singer, she feels compelled to assiduously _____ her albums and shows.
   A. intonate
   B. articulate
   C. harmonize
   D. promote
   E. ascertain

8. Annika found the _____ climate of Costa Rica preferable to the arid climate of Phoenix.
   A. unendurable
   B. festering
   C. sultry
   D. impaired
   E. sallow

1. **A.** *Compel* means *require. Ascertain* means *confirm, endure* means *bear, fester* means *get worse,* and *avenge* means *get revenge for.*

2. **E.** *Sultry* means *hot and humid. Eerie* means *spooky, disconsolate* means *miserable, buoyant* means *very excited,* and *sagacious* means *wise.*

3. **B.** *Unendurable* means *intolerable. Desolate* means *miserable, ebullient* means *very excited, intermittent* means *sporadic,* and *meager* means *little.*

4. **C.** *Intonation* and *inflection* mean *pitch.* Use the process of elimination. *Injunction, dictum,* and *writ* mean *formal declaration,* and *metamorphosis* means *change.*

5. **C.** "Fester means to get worse."
   - A. Ascertain (confirm) means to get indifferent (uncaring) . . . no.
   - B. Morph (change) means to get amalgamated (gathered together) . . . no, not necessarily.
   - C. Convalesce (heal) means to get better . . . yes!
   - D. Homogenize means to get varied . . . no, *homogenize* means to get *unified.*
   - E. Reel (stagger) means to get brittle (fragile) . . . no.

6. **D.** "Sultry (hot and humid) is the opposite of arid (dry)."
   - A. Eddies is the opposite of swirls . . . no, they are synonyms.
   - B. Cadence is the opposite of timber . . . no, they are synonyms.
   - C. Prolonged is the opposite of protracted . . . no, they are synonyms.
   - D. Secluded (alone) is the opposite of communal (together) . . . yes!
   - E. Stymie is the opposite of thwart . . . no, they both mean *block.*

7. **D.** "Even though Kirsten is already a successful professional singer, she feels compelled to assiduously *????* her albums and shows."

   Use the process of elimination. *Promote* means *advertise* or *publicize,* and is the best answer. Be careful of choices A, B, and C, which relate to singing, but do not fit the blank or the evidence and flow of the sentence. *Assiduously* means *diligently,* but you could get this question correct even if you didn't know that definition!

8. **C.** "Annika found the *not arid* climate of Costa Rica preferable to the arid climate of Phoenix."

   Sultry means *hot and* **humid,** which is the opposite of *arid* (dry).

Group 30
Sheer Menace

Find each of the following words on the *New Moon* page number provided. Based on the way each word is used in the book, guess at its definition.

1. **Sheer** (p. 359) might mean _____

   _____

2. **Buffeting** (p. 360) might mean _____

   _____

3. **Torrents** (p. 363) might mean _____

   _____

4. **Desolate** (p. 368) might mean _____

   _____

5. **Ramshackle** (p. 369) might mean _____

   _____

6. **Confide** (p. 370) might mean _____

   _____

7. **Listlessly** (p. 374) might mean _____

   _____

8. **Raking** (p. 377) might mean _____

   _____

Let's see how you did. Check your answers, write the exact definitions, and reread the sentence in *New Moon* where each word appears. Then complete the drills on the next page.

1. **Sheer** (p. 359) means *very steep*. It can also mean *absolute* or *very thin,* as in ultra-**sheer** stockings. This is another great example of a word with several meanings that the SAT, ACT, GED, or SSAT might use in a reading-comprehension question. The question might offer *very steep, absolute,* and *very thin* as answers, and you will have to decide which definition fits how the word is used in the context of the passage. For these questions on standardized tests, always reread a few sentences before and a few sentences after the word.

2. **Buffeting** (p. 360) means *battering*. You can see this a few sentences earlier: ". . . the **battering** of the current that flung me round and round like a rag doll."

3. **Torrents** (p. 363) means *large amounts of fast-moving water.*

4. **Desolate** (p. 368) means *miserable* or *deserted*. That's easy to remember; it even sounds like *deserted*. Bella is **miserable** because Edward **deserted** her.

5. **Ramshackle** (p. 369) means *run-down*. This was a synonym for *dilapidated* in Group 14. The other synonym was *decrepit*. *New Moon* Quiz 4: What item did Bella find that was **dilapidated** on page 126 of *New Moon?* What is the later significance of that item?

6. **Confide** (p. 370) means *tell the truth to* or *trust,* like having **confide**nce in someone's ability to keep a secret. Also, a *confidant* is a *trusted friend or ally.*

7. **Listlessly** (p. 374) means *with no energy*. Synonyms for *listless:* exhausted, lethargic, sluggish, weary, with lassitude, with torpor.

8. **Raking** (p. 377) in this case means *searching*. It can also mean *gathering with a rake, setting a stage floor at an angle,* or *moving in a sweeping motion,* like when Sam Uley, Charlie, Mr. Newton, and others were sweeping the woods looking for Bella after Edward left.

Synonyms: Select the word or phrase whose meaning is closest to the word in capital letters.

125

1. SHEER
   A. erratic
   B. vertical
   C. capricious
   D. impulsive
   E. mercurial

2. TORRENTS
   A. intonations
   B. inflections
   C. floods
   D. remnants
   E. injunctions

3. DESOLATE
   A. deserted
   B. ramshackle
   C. buffeting
   D. dilapidated
   E. listless

4. RAKING
   A. exhausted
   B. lethargic
   C. solemn
   D. somber
   E. searching

Analogies: Select the answer choice that best completes the meaning of the sentence.

5. Ramshackle is to dilapidated as
   A. listless is to steep
   B. confidant is to ally
   C. weary is to compelled
   D. eerie is to festering
   E. sultry is to intermittent

6. Lethargic is to energy as
   A. desolate is to misery
   B. listless is to torpor
   C. weary is to lassitude
   D. sophomoric is to naiveté
   E. fickle is to consistency

Sentence Completions: Choose the word or words that, when inserted in the sentence, best fits the meaning of the sentence as a whole.

7. When Jacob revved the old _____ motorcycle, the motor barely worked and only _____ sputtered.
   A. dilapidated .. compellingly
   B. impulsive .. sluggishly
   C. run-down .. listlessly
   D. ramshackle .. unremittingly
   E. mechanical .. patently

8. Tristan desperately _____ the crowd, searching for the one person he desired to find.
   A. compelled
   B. ascertained
   C. avenged
   D. raked
   E. chastised

1. **B.** Even if you might not have thought of *sheer* meaning *vertical,* it is the *best* choice. Sometimes standardized tests do that; they give a choice that is not perfect, but is better than the others and is therefore the correct answer. *Erratic, capricious, impulsive,* and *mercurial* mean *changing too easily.*

2. **C.** *Torrents* means *floods. Intonations* and *inflections* mean *pitches, remnants* means *leftovers,* and *injunctions* means *formal declarations.*

3. **A.** *Desolate* can mean *deserted. Ramshackle* and *dilapidated* mean *run-down, buffeting* means *battering,* and *listless* means *lacking energy.*

4. **E.** *Raking* can mean *searching.* Use the process of elimination. *Exhausted* and *lethargic* mean *lacking energy,* and *solemn* and *somber* mean *serious.*

5. **B.** "Ramshackle (run-down) is a synonym of dilapidated (run-down)."

   A. Listless (lacking energy) is a synonym of steep . . . no.
   B. Confidant (trusted friend) is a synonym of ally . . . yes!
   C. Weary is a synonym of compelled . . . no.
   D. Eerie is a synonym of festering (getting worse) . . . no.
   E. Sultry (hot and humid) is a synonym of intermittent (sporadic) . . . no.

6. **E.** "Lethargic means to lack energy."

   A. Desolate (miserable) means to lack misery . . . no.
   B. Listless means to lack torpor (fatigue) . . . no.
   C. Weary means to lack lassitude (fatigue) . . . no.
   D. Sophomoric (childish) means to lack naiveté (innocence) . . . no.
   E. Fickle (inconsistent) means to lack consistency . . . yes!

7. **C.** "When Jacob revved the old <u>old</u> motorcycle, the motor barely worked and only <u>barely</u> sputtered."

   Use the process of elimination, one blank at a time. Watch out for *mechanical* in choice E, which relates to motorcycles, but not directly to the evidence ("old" and "barely worked") in the sentence. Did you remember the word *patently* in choice E? It is a great synonym for *overtly* from Group 23 and means *obviously.*

8. **D.** "Tristan desperately <u>searched</u> the crowd, searching for the one person he desired to find."

   Raked means *searched.*

Quiz 6

I. Let's review some of the words that you've seen in Groups 26–30. Match each of the following words to the correct definition or synonym on the right. Then check the solutions on page 172.

1. Solemn		A.	Fuse
2. Coalesce		B.	Mandate
3. Rapt		C.	Desolate
4. Injunction		D.	Somber
5. Timid		E.	Censure
6. Chastise		F.	Captivated
7. Wretched		G.	Hot and humid
8. Exultant		H.	Pusillanimous
9. Scant		I.	Steep
10. Sultry		J.	With lassitude
11. Unendurable		K.	Ebullient
12. Intonation		L.	Negligible
13. Sheer		M.	Childish
14. Listless		N.	Inflection
15. Sophomoric		O.	Intolerable

II. Let's review several of the word parts that you've seen in Groups 26–30. Match each of the following word parts to the correct definition or synonym on the right. Then check the solutions on page 172.

16. In-		A.	Shape
17. Meta-		B.	Across
18. Morph-		C.	Not
19. Homo-		D.	Together
20. Trans-		E.	Change
21. Co-		F.	Same

Allegiance?

Find each of the following words on the *New Moon* page number provided. Based on the way each word is used in the book, guess at its definition.

1. **Autophile** (p. 378) might mean _____

   _____

2. **Aghast** (p. 378) might mean _____

   _____

3. **Congealing** (p. 379) might mean _____

   _____

4. **Attuned** (p. 384) might mean _____

   _____

5. **Perplexity** (p. 385) might mean _____

   _____

6. **Allegiance** (p. 386) might mean _____

   _____

7. **Oblivion** (p. 395) might mean _____

   _____

8. **Belligerent** (p. 397) might mean _____

   _____

Let's see how you did. Check your answers, write the exact definitions, and reread the sentence in *New Moon* where each word appears. Then complete the drills on the next page.

1. **Autophile** (p. 378) means *car lover.* The word part *phil-* means *lover of,* and of course *auto-* in this case is short for *automobile. Phil-* buys you so many great SAT, ACT, GED, and SSAT vocabulary words, such as *philosophy* (love of wisdom), *philanthropist* (one who loves humans and donates money to help charities), *bibliophile* (one who loves books), *audiophile* (one who loves stereo equipment), and even *Philadelphia* (the city of brotherly love).

2. **Aghast** (p. 378) means *horrified,* like you've seen a ghost. This reminds me of the word *ghastly,* meaning *gruesome,* which was a synonym for *macabre* in Group 7.

3. **Congealing** (p. 379) means *coming together.* Remember that *con-* means *together,* so this word means *gelling together*—definitely a word that means what it sounds like. This is another terrific synonym for *coalescing* from Group 26. The other synonyms were *amalgamating, converging, fusing,* and *homogenizing.*

4. **Attuned** (p. 384) means *in tune with,* and is yet another word that means what it sounds like.

5. **Perplexity** (p. 385) means *confusion.*

6. **Allegiance** (p. 386) means *loyalty.* Here it is—time to choose sides . . . Team Edward or Team Jacob? Synonym: fidelity.

7. **Oblivion** (p. 395) means *unconsciousness.* It can also mean *death* or *extinction,* like when Riff Raff says, "Exactly, Dr. Scott. And now, Frank N. Furter, your time has come. Say goodbye to all of this . . . and hello to **oblivion.**" (Twentieth Century Fox, *The Rocky Horror Picture Show,* 1975)

8. **Belligerent** (p. 397) means *hostile and aggressive.* A great synonym is *bellicose.* Both of these words come from the Latin word *bellum* for *war.* Don't worry, this word has no relation to **Bella Swan,** which means *beautiful swan.* Other incredible SAT, ACT, GED, and SSAT synonyms are *pugnacious* and *truculent.*

Synonyms: Select the word or phrase whose meaning is closest to the word in capital letters.

1. PHILANTHROPIST
   A. sage
   B. donor
   C. confidant
   D. coven
   E. albino

2. CONGEAL
   A. attune
   B. obliterate
   C. buffet
   D. confide
   E. amalgamate

3. ALLEGIANCE
   A. fidelity
   B. compel
   C. ascertain
   D. endure
   E. avenge

4. BELLIGERENT
   A. eerie
   B. festering
   C. bellicose
   D. haggard
   E. nebulous

Analogies: Select the answer choice that best completes the meaning of the sentence.

5. Pugnacious is to hostile as
   A. attuned is to aghast
   B. congealing is to perplexed
   C. blatant is to surreptitious
   D. truculent is to aggressive
   E. petulant is to supple

6. Bibliophile is to books as
   A. Edwardphile is to Jacob
   B. audiophile is to stereo equipment
   C. Francophile is to stamps
   D. vampophile is to werewolves
   E. philosopher is to soccer

Sentence Completions: Choose the word or words that, when inserted in the sentence, <u>best</u> fits the meaning of the sentence as a whole.

7. Not as composed as her sister, Edwina became _____ when angered.
   A. equanimous
   B. furtive
   C. reticent
   D. serene
   E. belligerent

8. Harry was _____ when the plans of the dark lord began _____ in his mind and he understood the extent of the villainy.
   A. elated .. coming together
   B. aghast .. raking
   C. perplexed .. corresponding
   D. horrified .. congealing
   E. attuned .. infiltrating

1. **B.** *Philanthropist* means *a person who helps others, usually by **donating** to charities,* so choice B is best. The word breaks down to *phil-* (nothing to do with Bella's stepdad) meaning *love of,* and *anthro-,* which refers to *humans.*

2. **E.** *Congeal* and *amalgamate* mean *come together. Attune* means *tune in to, obliterate* means *destroy, buffet* can mean *batter,* and *confide* means *trust.*

3. **A.** *Allegiance* and *fidelity* mean *loyalty. Allegiance* even sounds like *ally. Compel* means *urge, ascertain* means *confirm, endure* means *bear,* and *avenge* means *get revenge for.*

4. **C.** *Belligerent* and *bellicose* mean *hostile and aggressive. Eerie* means *spooky, festering* means *getting worse, haggard* means *tired looking,* and *nebulous* means *unclear.*

5. **D.** "Pugnacious means hostile."
   A. Attuned (tuned in to) means aghast (horrified) . . . no, it depends on what you're tuned in to.
   B. Congealing (coming together) means perplexed (confused) . . . no.
   C. Blatant (obvious) means surreptitious (secretive) . . . no.
   D. Truculent means aggressive . . . yes.
   E. Petulant (irritable) means supple (flexible) . . . no.

6. **B.** "A bibliophile loves books."
   A. An Edwardphile loves Jacob . . . no, come on now.
   B. An audiophile loves stereo equipment . . . yes.
   C. A Francophile loves stamps . . . no, a Francophile is *someone who loves France;* a *philatelist* is *someone who loves stamps.*
   D. A vampophile loves werewolves . . . no, only one vampophile loves werewolves, and yes, I made that word up.
   E. A philosopher loves soccer . . . no, not necessarily.

7. **E.** "Not as composed as her sister, Edwina became <u>not composed</u> when angered."
   Notice that the word you want for the blank is the opposite of *composed* in the first part of the sentence—the opposition words "not as _____ as . . . " give that away. *Belligerent* means *hostile* and fits best. *Equanimous* and *serene* mean *composed,* but you want the opposite.

8. **D.** "Harry was <u>upset</u> when the plans of the dark lord began <u>clarifying</u> in his mind and he understood the extent of the villainy."
   If you can't think of a word to fill a blank, decide if the word should be positive or negative, and then use the process of elimination, one blank at a time. *Horrified* means *upset,* and *congealing* means *coming together.*

An Egregious Lapse

Find each of the following words on the *New Moon* page number provided. Based on the way each word is used in the book, guess at its definition.

1. **Charade** (p. 400) might mean _____

_____

2. **Egregious** (p. 403) might mean _____

_____

3. **Lapse** (p. 403) might mean _____

_____

4. **Foresight** (p. 403) might mean _____

_____

5. **Antagonism** (p. 406) might mean _____

_____

6. **Metaphorically** (p. 410) might mean _____

_____

7. **Protocol** (p. 411) might mean _____

_____

8. **Mundane** (p. 411) might mean _____

_____

Let's see how you did. Check your answers, write the exact definitions,
and reread the sentence in *New Moon* where each word appears. Then
complete the drills on the next page.

1. **Charade** (p. 400) means *false display,* like the game **charades,** in
   which one player mimes a word or phrase, such as "McLovin's
   lava lamp," that others try to guess. Synonyms: facade, farce, hoax,
   pretense, ruse, sham. You can play *Twilight* charades. Write down
   fifteen main characters on slips of paper and drop them into a jar.
   Players take turns picking a slip of paper and silently imitating the
   character while others try to guess it.

2. **Egregious** (p. 403) means *very bad.*

3. **Lapse** (p. 403) means *failure* or *mistake.*

4. **Foresight** (p. 403) means *seeing into the future.* Remember from
   Group 22 that *fore-* means *in front,* and that's why *foresight*
   means *seeing in front or before something happens.* In Group 8, you
   had *premonition,* which means *a warning before something happens.*
   Synonyms: foreboding, intuition, presentiment.

5. **Antagonism** (p. 406) means *hostility.* Synonyms: acrimony,
   animosity, animus, antipathy, enmity, rancor.

6. **Metaphorically** (p. 410) means *symbolically.* Bella won't really die
   when Alice leaves, but the expression is a **symbol** for how strongly
   she feels.

7. **Protocol** (p. 411) means *code of behavior.* In case you're a *Star Wars*
   fan, C-3PO is a **protocol** droid, which means that he translates
   languages and suggests proper **etiquette** in meetings between
   different cultures. Synonyms: convention, decorum, etiquette,
   propriety.

8. **Mundane** (p. 411) means *ordinary.* It comes from the Latin word
   mundus, meaning *world,* and refers to *of **this** world* (ordinary),
   rather than *of heaven* (extraordinary). Perhaps the word *muggle*
   (an **ordinary**, unimaginative, and dull person, like Dudley, Aunt
   Petunia, or Uncle Vernon) comes from the same root word.

Synonyms: Select the word or phrase whose meaning is closest to the word in capital letters.

1. CHARADE
   A. lapse
   B. ruse
   C. metaphor
   D. fidelity
   E. oblivion

2. ANTAGONISM
   A. acrimony
   B. foresight
   C. presentiment
   D. decorum
   E. propriety

3. PROTOCOL
   A. facade
   B. farce
   C. hoax
   D. pretense
   E. convention

4. MUNDANE
   A. egregious
   B. symbolic
   C. ordinary
   D. fusing
   E. perplexed

Analogies: Select the answer choice that best completes the meaning of the sentence.

5. Extraordinary is to mundane as
   A. animosity is to trivial
   B. animus is to remote
   C. antipathy is to imperious
   D. enmity is to solicitous
   E. rancor is to macabre

6. Flawless is to lapse as
   A. mundane is to remnant
   B. attuned is to edict
   C. perplexing is to castanet
   D. aplomb is to truculence
   E. sophomoric is to reverberation

Sentence Completions: Choose the word or words that, when inserted in the sentence, <u>best</u> fits the meaning of the sentence as a whole.

7. Sierra realized that not trusting Monique's intuition had been _____ mistake; she would have been far better off if she had taken Monique's counsel.
   A. a metaphorical
   B. a mundane
   C. an egregious
   D. an attuned
   E. a philanthropic

8. The governor believed that his deputy's break in protocol was a mere _____ in judgment, not an intentional act of _____.
   A. error .. etiquette
   B. charade .. hostility
   C. lapse .. antagonism
   D. ruse .. belligerence
   E. intonation .. truculence

1. **B.** *Charade* and *ruse* mean *false display*. *Lapse* means *error, metaphor*
   means *symbol, fidelity* means *loyalty,* and *oblivion* means *unconsciousness.*
2. **A.** *Antagonism* and *acrimony* mean *hostility*. *Foresight* and
   presentiment mean *seeing before,* and *decorum* and *propriety* mean *code
   of proper behavior.*
3. **E.** *Protocol* and *convention* mean *code of behavior*. *Facade, farce, hoax,*
   and *pretense* mean *false display*. Use the process of elimination,
   and make sure to try all the choices. You may think of *protocol*
   as a *false display,* but that is debatable, and *convention* is the most
   direct synonym.
4. **C.** *Mundane* means *ordinary*. Use the process of elimination–cross
   off answers that you are **sure** don't work and choose the best of
   what's left. *Egregious* means *very bad,* and *fusing* means *joining*.
5. **D.** "Extraordinary is the opposite of mundane (ordinary)."
   Check out all these amazing words that you've learned!
   - A. Animosity (hostility) is the opposite of trivial
     (unimportant) . . . no.
   - B. Animus (hostility) is the opposite of remote (far away) . . . no.
   - C. Antipathy (hostility) is the opposite of imperious (bossy) . . .
     no.
   - (D.) Enmity (hostility) is the opposite of solicitous (concerned) . . .
     maybe.
   - E. Rancor (hostility) is the opposite of macabre (grim) . . . no.
     Using the process of elimination, choice D is the best answer.
6. **D.** "Flawless means no lapse (error)."
   - A. Mundane (ordinary) means no remnant (left over) . . . no.
   - B. Attuned (tuned in to) means no edict (formal declaration) . . .
     no.
   - C. Perplexing (confusing) means no castanet (percussion
     instrument) . . . no.
   - (D.) Aplomb (calm) means no truculence (aggressive hostility) . . .
     yes!
   - E. Sophomoric (childish) means no reverberation (echo) . . . no.
7. **C.** "Sierra realized that not trusting Monique's intuition had
   been *a bad* mistake; she would have been far better off if she had
   taken Monique's counsel."
   Egregious means *very bad*. Choice B, *mundane* (ordinary), does
   not work because the sentence tells you that she would have
   been "far better off" if she had taken Monique's advice.
8. **C.** "The governor believed that his deputy's break in protocol
   was a mere *break* in judgment, not an intentional act of *rudeness*."
   Choice C, *lapse* (error) and *antagonism* (hostility), fits best.

Transgressing

Find each of the following words on the *New Moon* page number provided. Based on the way each word is used in the book, guess at its definition.

1. **Sporadically** (p. 419) might mean _____

    _____

2. **Tabulated** (p. 420) might mean _____

    _____

3. **Apt** (p. 429) might mean _____

    _____

4. **Transitory** (p. 429) might mean _____

    _____

5. **Formidable** (p. 429) might mean _____

    _____

6. **Millennia** (p. 429) might mean _____

    _____

7. **Transgressors** (p. 430) might mean _____

    _____

8. **Flout** (p. 430) might mean _____

    _____

Let's see how you did. Check your answers, write the exact definitions, 137
and reread the sentence in *New Moon* where each word appears. Then
complete the drills on the next page.

1. **Sporadically** (p. 419) means *occasionally.* Synonym: intermittently.

2. **Tabulated** (p. 420) means *calculated.* It is actually just the word
   table (as in *mathematical chart*) with the ending *-ate,* which makes it
   a verb—*the action of adding up items in a table.*

3. **Apt** (p. 429) means *appropriate, likely,* or *able.* You saw this word in
   Group 24 as a synonym for *able.* This is another perfect example
   of a simple word with several meanings that the SAT, ACT,
   GED, or SSAT would ask you to determine the meaning of from
   context. Learning to define words from their context, like you are
   doing here with *New Moon,* is a great skill! Synonyms: apposite,
   apropos, germane, pertinent.

4. **Transitory** (p. 429) means *changing* or *impermanent.* Alice, always
   looking out for your test scores, defines the word right after she
   says it. "Others are more . . . transitory. It **changes.**" Remember
   from Group 26 that *trans-* means *across,* and that's why *transitory*
   means *moving across—changing.* Synonyms: ephemeral, evanescent,
   transient. I saw *evanescent* on a recent ACT. It stumped most
   students, but now it won't stump you!

5. **Formidable** (p. 429) means *very powerful.* Alice defines the word
   by saying ". . . gifts that make what I can do look like a parlor
   trick." Standardized tests always do that, too; they define difficult
   words nearby in the passage. *New Moon* Quiz 5: Who in the
   vampire world, would you say, has the most **formidable** gift?

6. **Millennia** (p. 429) means *thousands of years.* It's the plural of
   millennium (one thousand years).

7. **Transgressors** (p. 430) means *rule breakers.* You had that word
   in Group 26 when you first learned *trans-.* It means *people who go
   across boundaries—break rules.*

8. **Flout** (p. 430) means *disobey* or *disregard.*

Synonyms: Select the word or phrase whose meaning is closest to the word in capital letters.

1. SPORADIC
   A. intermittent
   B. tabulated
   C. formidable
   D. ephemeral
   E. egregious

2. APT
   A. transient
   B. mundane
   C. germane
   D. oblivious
   E. bellicose

3. TRANSITORY
   A. interminable
   B. incessant
   C. perpetual
   D. unremitting
   E. evanescent

4. FLOUT
   A. prolong
   B. disregard
   C. stymie
   D. thwart
   E. placate

Analogies: Select the answer choice that best completes the meaning of the sentence.

5. Apt is to pertinent as
   A. sporadic is to sheer
   B. egregious is to ramshackle
   C. mundane is to ordinary
   D. aghast is to listless
   E. homogenized is to sultry

6. Transgressors is to flout as
   A. lawyers is to infiltrate
   B. judges is to rebuke
   C. Charlie is to infuses
   D. police is to enforce
   E. vampires is to bite

Sentence Completions: Choose the word that, when inserted in the sentence, best fits the meaning of the sentence as a whole.

7. Fatima _____ her grade-point average and realized that she could get a B on the History final exam and still have an A average.
   A. flouted
   B. transgressed
   C. tabulated
   D. reprimanded
   E. admonished

8. Long before humans arrived, dinosaurs thrived for _____ until they mysteriously became extinct.
   A. millennia
   B. virtues
   C. mutations
   D. twilight
   E. mystification

1. **A.** *Sporadic* and *intermittent* mean *occasional*. *Tabulated* means *calculated*, *formidable* means *very powerful*, *ephemeral* means *temporary*, and *egregious* means *very bad*.

2. **C.** *Apt* and *germane* mean *appropriate*. *Transient* means *temporary*, *mundane* means *ordinary*, *oblivious* means *unaware*, and *bellicose* means *aggressively hostile*.

3. **E.** *Transitory* and *evanescent* mean *temporary*. *Interminable, incessant, perpetual*, and *unremitting* mean *endless*.

4. **B.** *Flout* means *disregard*. *Prolong* means *make longer*. *Stymie* and *thwart* mean *prevent*, and *placate* means *soothe*.

5. **C.** "Apt means pertinent."
   A. Sporadic (occasional) means sheer (steep) . . . no.
   B. Egregious (very bad) means ramshackle (run-down) . . . no.
   C. Mundane means ordinary . . . yes.
   D. Aghast (horrified) means listless (lacking energy) . . . no.
   E. Homogenized (unified) means sultry (hot and humid) . . . no.

6. **D.** "Transgressors flout the law."
   A. Lawyers infiltrate (enter) the law . . . no, that makes no sense.
   B. Judges rebuke (scold) the law . . . no, they rebuke criminals.
   C. Charlie infuses (mixes) the law . . . no, that makes no sense.
   D. The police enforce the law . . . yes!
   E. Vampires bite the law . . . no, they do bite, but not the law.
   If your sentence was "Transgressors flout" and several answer choices worked, make the sentence more specific. Don't convince yourself that a choice that does not make sense to you is correct; choose an answer that has a clear relationship.

7. **C.** "Fatima _determined_ her grade-point average and realized that she could get a B on the History final exam and still have an A average."
   Use the process of elimination. *Tabulated* means *calculated* and works best.

8. **A.** "Long before humans arrived, dinosaurs thrived for _many years_ until they mysteriously became extinct."
   Millennia means *thousands of years*.

Group 34
Imminent Landing

Find each of the following words on the *New Moon* page number provided. Based on the way each word is used in the book, guess at its definition.

1. **Annihilating** (p. 431) might mean _____
   _____

2. **Mavericks** (p. 431) might mean _____
   _____

3. **Stupor** (p. 433) might mean _____
   _____

4. **Intrigued** (p. 435) might mean _____
   _____

5. **Writhing** (p. 436) might mean _____
   _____

6. **Imminent** (p. 439) might mean _____
   _____

7. **Scourge** (p. 440) might mean _____
   _____

8. **Sardonic** (p. 441) might mean _____
   _____

Let's see how you did. Check your answers, write the exact definitions, and reread the sentences in *New Moon* where each word appears. Then complete the drills on the next page.

1. **Annihilating** (p. 431) means *completely destroying.* This word comes from *nihil-,* meaning *nothing,* so *annihilating* means *reduce to* **nothing.** Synonyms: eradicating, obliterating.

2. **Mavericks** (p. 431) are *people who do not follow societies' rules.* Synonyms: dissenters, dissidents, nonconformists.

3. **Stupor** (p. 433) means *dazed state* or *unconsciousness.* This word can mean the same thing as *oblivion* from Group 31. Although whereas *stupor* only refers to a *dazed state, oblivion* can also mean *annihilation.*

4. **Intrigued** (p. 435) means *curious* or *interested.*

5. **Writhing** (p. 436) means *twisting* or *squirming.* This word has the same root as *wreath,* which is *a decoration made of branches interwoven and **twisted** together.*

6. **Imminent** (p. 439) means *occurring soon.* My math teacher in high school used to say, "A quiz is imminent," meaning "You had better study." Synonyms: forthcoming, impending, looming.

7. **Scourge** (p. 440) means *problem* or *plague.* This means the same thing as *bane* from Group 15. Another great synonym is *affliction.*

8. **Sardonic** (p. 441) means *sarcastic.* In the cable television show *Monk,* Monk's brilliant brother, Ambrose, defines *sardonic* by saying, "You were being **sardonic.** Sarcasm is a contemptuous ironic statement. You were being mockingly derisive. That's **sardonic.**" (USA Cable Network, *Monk,* "Mr. Monk and the Three Pigs," 2002) He means that *sardonic* is a bit meaner than *sarcastic.* Technically he's right, but the SAT, ACT, GED, SSAT, and most people use them as synonyms. Monk and his brother do tend to be a *bit* particular about things.

Synonyms: Select the word or phrase whose meaning is closest to the word in capital letters.

1. MAVERICK
   A. autophile
   B. confidant
   C. sadist
   D. nonconformist
   E. canine

2. STUPOR
   A. exposition
   B. oblivion
   C. communism
   D. curriculum
   E. exasperation

3. IMMINENT
   A. writhing
   B. intrigued
   C. annihilated
   D. impending
   E. eradicated

4. SARDONIC
   A. sarcastic
   B. sporadic
   C. intermittent
   D. apposite
   E. apropos

Analogies: Select the answer choice that best completes the meaning of the sentence.

5. Imminent is to remote as
   A. forthcoming is to impending
   B. looming is to sporadic
   C. transitory is to transient
   D. intermittent is to incessant
   E. egregious is to mundane

6. Solicitous is to intrigued as
   A. writhing is to squirming
   B. formidable is to sheer
   C. rancorous is to desolate
   D. aghast is to ramshackle
   E. truculent is to mercurial

Sentence Completions: Choose the word or words that, when inserted in the sentence, best fits the meaning of the sentence as a whole.

7. Ms. Darbus _____ cell phones and considered them the _____ of the times.
   A. loved .. affliction
   B. liked .. bane
   C. hated .. scourge
   D. tabulated .. impasse
   E. mimicked .. eventuality

8. After a full day of school, basketball practice, and SAT class, the students fell onto the couch in an exhausted _____.
   A. stupor
   B. reverie
   C. contingency
   D. precipice
   E. compulsion

1. **D.** *Maverick* means *nonconformist. Autophile* means *car lover,* *confidant* means *trusted friend, sadist* means *a person who is intentionally cruel,* and *canine* means *dog-like.*

2. **B.** *Stupor* and *oblivion* mean *unconsciousness. Exposition* means *explanation, communism* is *a political philosophy, curriculum* means *plan of study,* and *exasperation* means *frustration.*

3. **D.** *Imminent* and *impending* mean *about to happen. Writhing* means *squirming, intrigued* means *curious,* and *annihilated* and *eradicated* mean *destroyed.*

4. **A.** *Sardonic* means *sarcastic. Sporadic* and *intermittent* mean *occasional,* and *apposite* and *apropos* mean *appropriate.*

5. **D.** "Imminent (about to happen) is the opposite of remote (far away)."
   - A. Forthcoming (about to happen) is the opposite of impending (about to happen) . . . no.
   - B. Looming (about to happen) is the opposite of sporadic (occasional) . . . no, not quite.
   - C. Transitory (temporary) is the opposite of transient (temporary) . . . no.
   - (D.) Intermittent (occasional) is the opposite of incessant (constant) . . . yes!
   - E. Egregious (very bad) is the opposite of mundane (ordinary) . . . maybe, but choice D is clearer and the words are direct opposites.

6. **A.** "Solicitous (interested) is similar to intrigued."
   - (A.) Writhing is similar to squirming . . . yes!
   - B. Formidable (very powerful) is similar to sheer (steep) . . . no.
   - C. Rancorous (hostile) is similar to desolate (miserable) . . . no.
   - D. Aghast (horrified) is similar to ramshackle (run-down) . . . no.
   - E. Truculent (hostile) is similar to mercurial (erratic) . . . no.

7. **C.** "Ms. Darbus *????* cell phones and considered them the *????* of the times."
   This is the rare type of sentence-completion question, like you saw in Group 21, where you do not have any information to determine a word for each blank. For this type of question, determine if the words should be similar or opposite. Once you decide, examine the choices and use the process of elimination. Here the words need to be similar, either both positive or both negative, so choice C is the only one that fits.

8. **A.** "After a full day of school, basketball practice, and SAT class, the students fell onto the couch in an exhausted *exhaustion.*"
   Stupor means *exhaustion.*

Through the Throngs

Find each of the following words on the *New Moon* page number provided. Based on the way each word is used in the book, guess at its definition.

1. **Sienna** (p. 442) might mean _____

   _____

2. **Billowed** (p. 444) might mean _____

   _____

3. **Crimson** (p. 444) might mean _____

   _____

4. **Throngs** (p. 445) might mean _____

   _____

5. **Distended** (p. 448) might mean _____

   _____

6. **Edifice** (p. 450) might mean _____

   _____

7. **Leer** (p. 454) might mean _____

   _____

8. **Androgynous** (p. 456) might mean _____

   _____

Let's see how you did. Check your answers, write the exact definitions, and reread the sentence in *New Moon* where each word appears. Then complete the drills on the next page.

1. **Sienna** (p. 442) usually means *yellowish-brown,* like Edward's *ocher-*colored eyes. It can also refer to *reddish-brown,* like Jacob's *russet-*colored skin. Edward or Jacob? The movie might tell us which one Stephenie Meyer had in mind . . .

2. **Billowed** (p. 444) means *filled with air,* like the sail of a boat.

3. **Crimson** (p. 444) means *purplish-red.* Interestingly, so far in this Group you have *sienna* and *crimson* (yellowish-brown and purplish-red)—vegetarian and . . . well, . . . you know.

4. **Throngs** (p. 445) means *crowds.* Let's see that in context:
   " . . . the **throngs** of tourists passed, **crowding** the sidewalks, ... "
   In reading-comprehension questions, always base your answer on direct evidence in the passage; the correct answer will **always** have clear and direct evidence in the passage.

5. **Distended** (p. 448) means *stretched* or *swollen.* It even sounds like *extended—stretched.* Synonyms: bloated, engorged, protuberant.

6. **Edifice** (p. 450) means *building.* That's easy to remember since in Spanish *building* is *edificio.*

7. **Leer** (p. 454) in this case means an *unpleasant or even hostile look.* It can also mean an *inappropriately lustful look,* but I don't think Felix meant it that way—he sees Bella as only a human, meaning lunch. And anyway, Edward would not have stood for it. Synonyms: ogle, sneer. By the way, vocabulary aside, this is a sweet part of the book!

8. **Androgynous** (p. 456) means *not appearing clearly male or female.* Anime and manga often feature **androgynous** characters.

Synonyms: Select the word or phrase whose meaning is closest to the word in capital letters.

1. SIENNA
   A. alabaster
   B. burgundy
   C. ocher
   D. orange
   E. green

2. CRIMSON
   A. tawny
   B. purplish-red
   C. pallid
   D. sallow
   E. ashen

3. THRONG
   A. small bathing suit
   B. building
   C. unpleasant look
   D. crowd
   E. stupor

4. EDIFICE
   A. building
   B. scourge
   C. bane
   D. affliction
   E. millennia

Analogies: Select the answer choice that best completes the meaning of the sentence.

5. Distended is to stretched as
   A. androgynous is to anime
   B. transitory is to transgressed
   C. ephemeral is to tabulated
   D. evanescent is to intrigued
   E. eradicated is to obliterated

6. Wind is to billow as
   A. mavericks is to leer
   B. throngs is to distend
   C. jade is to crimson
   D. infection is to fester
   E. injunction is to imminent

Sentence Completions: Choose the word or words that, when inserted in the sentence, best fits the meaning of the sentence as a whole.

7. Cady, Regina, and Gretchen learned that they and the _____ of students at North Shore High School were happier when they replaced cruel _____ with friendly waves.
   A. throngs .. leers
   B. crowds .. smiles
   C. edifice .. sneers
   D. conviction .. ogles
   E. castanets .. grimaces

8. Characters in *manga,* a Japanese style of comics and animation, often appear _____; that is, they have both masculine and feminine characteristics.
   A. sienna
   B. crimson
   C. androgynous
   D. distended
   E. formidable

1. **C.** *Sienna* and *ocher* mean *yellowish-brown. Alabaster* means *white,* and *burgundy* means *dark purplish-red.*

2. **B.** *Crimson* means *purplish-red. Tawny* means *yellowish-brown. Pallid, sallow,* and *ashen* mean *pale.*

3. **D.** *Throng* means *crowd. Stupor* means *unconsciousness.*

4. **A.** *Edifice* means *building. Scourge* means *problem, bane* means *curse, affliction* means *ailment,* and *millennia* means *thousands of years.*

5. **E.** "Distended means stretched."
   - A. Androgynous (having masculine and feminine characteristics) means anime (Japanese animation) . . . no, but androgynous characters are drawn in anime.
   - B. Transitory (temporary) means transgressed (broke rules) . . . no.
   - C. Ephemeral (temporary) means tabulated (calculated) . . . no.
   - D. Evanescent (temporary) means intrigued (interested) . . . no.
   - (E.) Eradicated (destroyed) means obliterated (destroyed) . . . yes!

6. **D.** "Wind makes something billow."
   - A. Mavericks (free thinkers) make something leer (stare) . . . no.
   - B. Throngs (crowds) make something distend (swell) . . . no.
   - C. Jade (green) makes something crimson (purplish-red) . . . no.
   - (D.) An infection makes something fester (get worse) . . . yes.
   - E. An injunction (order) makes something imminent (happen soon) . . . maybe, but not as definitely as choice D.

7. **A.** "Cady, Regina, and Gretchen learned that they and the <u>tons</u> of students at North Shore High School were happier when they replaced cruel <u>waves</u> with friendly waves."

   Throngs means *crowds,* and *leers* can mean *nasty look,* so choice A is best.

8. **C.** "Characters in *manga,* a Japanese style of comics and animation, often appear <u>male and female looking;</u> that is, they have both masculine and feminine characteristics."

   Androgynous means *male and female looking.*

Quiz 7

I. Let's review some of the words that you've seen in Groups 31–35. Match each of the following words to the correct definition or synonym on the right. Then check the solutions on page 172.

1. Aghast	A. Like a muggle
2. Congealing	B. Very bad
3. Belligerent	C. Intermittent
4. Egregious	D. Fusing
5. Protocol	E. Horrified
6. Mundane	F. Bellicose
7. Sporadic	G. Dissenter
8. Apt	H. Sarcastic
9. Flout	I. Propriety
10. Maverick	J. Ogle
11. Imminent	K. Germane
12. Sardonic	L. Building
13. Throng	M. Disregard
14. Edifice	N. Crowd
15. Leer	O. Impending

II. Let's review several of the word parts that you've seen in Groups 31–35. Match each of the following word parts to the correct definition or synonym on the right. Then check the solutions on page 172.

16. Phil-	A. War
17. Bellum	B. In front
18. Con-	C. Across
19. Anthro-	D. Lover of
20. Fore-	E. Together
21. Trans-	F. Human

Group 36
Surreal

Find each of the following words on the *New Moon* page number provided. Based on the way each word is used in the book, guess at its definition.

1. **Subterranean** (p. 459) might mean _____

_____

2. **Ebony** (p. 460) might mean _____

_____

3. **Ghoulish** (p. 462) might mean _____

_____

4. **Contemptuous** (p. 465) might mean _____

_____

5. **Antechamber** (p. 465) might mean _____

_____

6. **Cavernous** (p. 465) might mean _____

_____

7. **Turret** (p. 465) might mean _____

_____

8. **Surreal** (p. 466) might mean _____

_____

Let's see how you did. Check your answers, write the exact definitions, and reread the sentence in *New Moon* where each word appears. Then complete the drills on the next page.

1. **Subterranean** (p. 459) means *underground. Terra-* means *earth,* and *sub-* means *below,* so *subterranean* just means *below earth— underground.* Here are a few other great *terra* words: *extraterrestrial* (*extra-* means *beyond,* so *beyond the Earth*), *territory* (area of land), and *terrain* (type of land).

2. **Ebony** (p. 460) means *black.* Let's review the color words that you've seen so far: *alabaster* (white), *blanched* (white), *crimson* (purplish-red), *jade* (green), *ocher* (yellowish-brown), *russet* (reddish-brown), *sienna* (reddish-brown), *tawny* (yellowish-brown), and now *ebony* (black). Use these terms to spice up your creative or descriptive essays in school. They are more interesting and more specific than the mundane primary colors. Plus, now you'll know what to expect if you order clothes from a catalog.

3. **Ghoulish** (p. 462) means *disturbing and unpleasant,* like a ghoul, and like the *South Park* Halloween episode when Phillip dresses as a ghost and says, "That fart was absolutely **ghoulish,** Terrance." (Comedy Central, "South Park," *Spooky Fish,* 1997) Synonyms: ghastly, grisly, grotesque, macabre, morbid.

4. **Contemptuous** (p. 465) means *angry and disobedient.* The ending *-ous* just means *characterized by,* so *contemptuous* means *characterized by contempt* (anger and disobedience). Synonyms for *contempt:* abhorrence, derision, disdain, scorn.

5. **Antechamber** (p. 465) means *entry room that precedes a larger room.* That's easy to break apart. *Ante-* means *before,* like the money you toss into the pot **before** a hand of poker. So *antechamber* means *before chamber—the small room that precedes a larger one.*

6. **Cavernous** (p. 465) means *very spacious,* like a big cavern. Great SAT, ACT, GED, and SSAT synonyms: capacious, voluminous.

7. **Turret** (p. 465) in this case means *a cylindrical tower on a corner or wall of a castle.*

8. **Surreal** (p. 466) means *unreal.*

Synonyms: Select the word or phrase whose meaning is closest to the word in capital letters.

1. SUBTERRANEAN
   - A. underground
   - B. extraterrestrial
   - C. ghoulish
   - D. morbid
   - E. macabre

2. EBONY
   - A. capacious
   - B. surreal
   - C. black
   - D. alabaster
   - E. tawny

3. CONTEMPTUOUS
   - A. distended
   - B. protuberant
   - C. engorged
   - D. scornful
   - E. voluminous

4. CAVERNOUS
   - A. disdainful
   - B. derisive
   - C. intermittent
   - D. haggard
   - E. capacious

Analogies: Select the answer choice that best completes the meaning of the sentence.

5. Turret is to castle as
   - A. ebony is to color
   - B. kismet is to fate
   - C. remnants are to original
   - D. carcass is to cadaver
   - E. smirk is to expression

6. Antechamber is to edifice as
   - A. taboo is to forbidden
   - B. preface is to book
   - C. edict is to formal
   - D. jade is to gemstone
   - E. hysteria is to panic

Sentence Completions: Choose the word that, when inserted in the sentence, best fits the meaning of the sentence as a whole.

7. The keys of a piano alternate between _____ and ivory—black and white.
   - A. sienna
   - B. alabaster
   - C. russet
   - D. ebony
   - E. tawny

8. In a court of law, judges will not tolerate _____ behavior and quickly call transgressors to order.
   - A. serpentine
   - B. inexorable
   - C. prophetic
   - D. rapacious
   - E. contemptuous

1. **A.** *Subterranean* means *underground*. *Extraterrestrial* means *from beyond Earth*, and *ghoulish, morbid,* and *macabre* mean *disturbing*.

2. **C.** *Ebony* means *black*. *Capacious* means *spacious*, *surreal* means *not real*, *alabaster* means *white*, and *tawny* means *yellowish-brown*.

3. **D.** *Contemptuous* and *scornful* mean *angry and disobedient*. *Distended, protuberant,* and *engorged* mean *swelled*, and *voluminous* means *spacious*.

4. **E.** Use the process of elimination. *Cavernous* and *capacious* mean *spacious*. *Disdainful* and *derisive* mean *scornful, intermittent* means *sporadic*, and *haggard* means *tired-looking*.

5. **C.** "A turret (tower) is part of a castle."
   A. Ebony (black) is part of a color . . . no, ebony is a type of color.
   B. Kismet is part of a fate . . . no, *kismet* means *fate*.
   C. Remnants are part of an original . . . maybe, it's what's left over.
   D. A carcass (dead animal body) is part of a cadaver (dead human body) . . . no!
   E. A smirk is part of an expression . . . no, a smirk is a type of expression.
   This type of relationship, "_____ is part of a _____," shows up quite a bit on the SSAT. Using the process of elimination, choice C is best.

6. **B.** "An antechamber is part of an edifice."
   A. Taboo is part of a forbidden . . . no, *taboo* means *forbidden*.
   B. A preface is part of a book . . . yes, and like an antechamber, it's the first part.
   C. An edict is part of a formal . . . no, an *edict* is *formal*.
   D. Jade is part of a gemstone . . . no, *jade* is *a green gemstone*.
   E. Hysteria is part of a panic . . . no, *hysteria* can mean *panic*.

7. **D.** "The keys of a piano alternate between <u>black</u> and ivory—black and white."
   Ebony means *black*.

8. **E.** "In a court of law, judges will not tolerate <u>transgressing</u> behavior and quickly call transgressors to order."
   Contemptuous means *angry and disobedient*, like *contempt of court*, and is the best answer. Let's review the other choices. *Serpentine* means *winding, inexorable* means *unstoppable, prophetic* means *predicting*, and *rapacious* means *very hungry or greedy*.

Group 37

Deference

Find each of the following words on the *New Moon* page number provided. Based on the way each word is used in the book, guess at its definition.

1. **Ecstatic** (p. 467) might mean _____

   _____

2. **Infallible** (p. 468) might mean _____

   _____

3. **Inure** (p. 472) might mean _____

   _____

4. **Siren** (p. 472) might mean _____

   _____

5. **Baleful** (p. 474) might mean _____

   _____

6. **Faux pas** (p. 474) might mean _____

   _____

7. **Entourage** (p. 474) might mean _____

   _____

8. **Deference** (p. 475) might mean _____

   _____

Let's see how you did. Check your answers, write the exact definitions, and reread the sentence in *New Moon* where each word appears. Then complete the drills on the next page.

1. **Ecstatic** (p. 467) means *very excited.* Are you getting bored by all of the words for *very excited?* You've had *exuberant, elated,* and *exultant* in Groups 15, 20, and 28, and their synonyms *buoyant, ebullient, euphoric, jubilant,* and *rapturous.* Standardized tests love these words; I bet one of them will be on your test!

2. **Infallible** (p. 468) means *always right—never wrong.*

3. **Inure** (p. 472) means *hold back.* Synonym: desensitize.

4. **Siren** (p. 472) means *alluring, but dangerous.* This word comes from a Greek myth about supernatural women who lured sailors to crash into rocks.

5. **Baleful** (p. 474) means *threatening.* You've seen this word as a synonym for *sinister, malevolent,* and *malicious* in Groups 9, 19, and 22. The other synonyms were *depraved, heinous, impious, iniquitous, menacing, nefarious,* and *pernicious. New Moon* Quiz 6: When was the last time you saw Edward this angry?

6. **Faux pas** (p. 474) means *violation of social rules—a social blunder,* like wiping your nose on your sleeve during a college interview. *Faux pas* literally translates from French as *false step.* This is a good time to review your recent word *protocol* and its synonyms, *convention, decorum, etiquette,* and *propriety,* which are *the social rules.*

7. **Entourage** (p. 474) can mean Turtle, Johnny Drama, E, and maybe even Ari, Lloyd, and the publicist, Shauna. It also means *the people around a famous or important person.* Synonyms: attendants, posse, retainers, retinue.

8. **Deference** (p. 475) means *giving in and showing respect.* Synonyms: acquiescence, compliance, obeisance, submission.

Synonyms: Select the word or phrase whose meaning is closest to the word in capital letters.

1. ECSTATIC
   A. ebullient
   B. menacing
   C. nefarious
   D. pernicious
   E. depraved

2. INFALLIBLE
   A. ghastly
   B. cavernous
   C. contemptuous
   D. perfect
   E. petulant

3. BALEFUL
   A. subterranean
   B. voluminous
   C. malevolent
   D. capacious
   E. distended

4. DEFERENCE
   A. entourage
   B. acquiescence
   C. enmity
   D. rancor
   E. animosity

Analogies: Select the answer choice that best completes the meaning of the sentence.

5. Compliance is to contempt as
   A. faux pas is to faux
   B. siren is to temptress
   C. euphoria is to heinous
   D. hysteria is to equanimity
   E. prolonged is to protracted

6. Entourage is to deference as
   A. attendants are to intonation
   B. posse is to avenging
   C. retainers are to shrewdness
   D. followers are to obeisance
   E. retinue is to homogenization

Sentence Completions: Choose the word that, when inserted in the sentence, best fits the meaning of the sentence as a whole.

7. Richard hoped that seeing Jayley regularly would _____ him to her charm and free him from his compulsion for her.
   A. siren
   B. inure
   C. billow
   D. distend
   E. obliterate

8. Em tried to convince James that she was a(n) _____, untrustworthy and dangerous.
   A. entourage
   B. remnant
   C. basilisk
   D. siren
   E. masochist

1. **A.** *Ecstatic* and *ebullient* mean *very excited. Menacing, nefarious, pernicious,* and *depraved* mean *threatening and sinister.*

2. **D.** *Infallible* means *perfect. Ghastly* means *disturbing, cavernous* means *spacious, contemptuous* means *angry and disobedient,* and *petulant* means *irritable.*

3. **C.** *Baleful* and *malevolent* mean *threatening. Subterranean* means *underground, voluminous* and *capacious* mean *spacious,* and *distended* means *swollen.*

4. **B.** *Deference* and *acquiescence* mean *giving in and showing respect. Entourage* means *group of followers;* and *enmity, rancor,* and *animosity* mean *hostility.*

5. **D.** "Compliance (following rules) is the opposite of contempt (disobedience)."
   A. Faux pas (social misstep) is the opposite of faux (fake) . . . no.
   B. Siren is the opposite of temptress . . . no, a *siren* is *a temptress.*
   C. Euphoria (being thrilled) is the opposite of heinous (wicked) . . . no.
   (D.) Hysteria (panic) is the opposite of equanimity (calm) . . . yes.
   E. Prolonged is the opposite of protracted . . . no, they both mean *made longer.*

6. **D.** "An entourage (followers) shows deference (respect)."
   A. Attendants show intonation (pitch) . . . no, that makes no sense.
   B. A posse (followers) shows avenging (getting revenge) . . . no.
   C. Retainers (followers) show shrewdness (cunning) . . . no.
   (D.) Followers show obeisance (obedience) . . . yes!
   E. A retinue (followers) shows homogenization (unifying) . . . maybe, but it's a stretch.

7. **B.** "Richard hoped that seeing Jayley regularly would _free/ desensitize_ him to her charm and free him from his compulsion for her."
   Inure means *desensitize.* "Free him" tells you that *inure* is the best answer.

8. **D.** "Em tried to convince James that she was a(n) _untrustworthy and dangerous person,_ untrustworthy and dangerous."
   Siren means *alluring and dangerous* and fits best. Em may have been a *masochist,* but *siren* more directly fits the evidence of "untrustworthy and dangerous."

Group 38

Subjective Visions?

Find each of the following words on the *New Moon* page number provided.
Based on the way each word is used in the book, guess at its definition.

1. **Confounds** (p. 476) might mean _____

_____

2. **Loathsome** (p. 479) might mean _____

_____

3. **Acquisitive** (p. 479) might mean _____

_____

4. **Fret** (p. 480) might mean _____

_____

5. **Subjective** (p. 480) might mean _____

_____

6. **Lustrous** (p. 483) might mean _____

_____

7. **Ornate** (p. 484) might mean _____

_____

8. **Opulent** (p. 485) might mean _____

_____

Let's see how you did. Check your answers, write the exact definitions, and reread the sentence in *New Moon* where each word appears. Then complete the drills on the next page.

1. **Confounds** (p. 476) means *stumps.* Synonyms: baffles, mystifies, perplexes.

2. **Loathsome** (p. 479) means *repulsive* or *worthy of hatred.* You can see this in the context. Bella questions, "Would he rather *die* than change me?" If someone would choose death over option two, then option two would have to be pretty **repulsive.** Incidentally, notice that Stephenie Meyer italicized "die" in that line. The SAT and ACT love to ask why a word in a passage is italicized. Usually (and in this case) it is to show that the word is emphasized when read.

3. **Acquisitive** (p. 479) in this case means *curious and greedy.* It can also just mean *greedy. Acquisitive* looks like *acquire,* and *acquisitive* can mean *wanting to **acquire** knowledge* (curious and greedy) or *wanting to **acquire** possessions* (greedy). The SAT and ACT often use the following synonyms for *acquisitive:* avaricious, covetous, rapacious.

4. **Fret** (p. 480) means *worry.*

5. **Subjective** (p. 480) means *dependent on a person's particular view.* There's a quote from a great old Mike Myers movie called *So I Married an Axe Murderer* that defines this word beautifully: "Well, *brutal*'s a very **subjective** word. I mean, what's brutal to one person might be totally reasonable to somebody else." (TriStar Pictures, 1993)

6. **Lustrous** (p. 483) means *shiny.* Synonyms: glossy, satiny.

7. **Ornate** (p. 484) means *decorated in a fancy way*—think of ornaments on a Christmas tree. Synonyms: adorned, elaborate, ornamented.

8. **Opulent** (p. 485) means *luxurious and showy.* Synonyms: grandiose, lavish, ostentatious, pretentious, sumptuous.

Synonyms: Select the word or phrase whose meaning is closest to the word in capital letters.

1. CONFOUND
   A. perplex
   B. fret
   C. inure
   D. billow
   E. distend

2. LOATHSOME
   A. acquisitive
   B. avaricious
   C. covetous
   D. rapacious
   E. repulsive

3. ORNATE
   A. baffling
   B. adorned
   C. mystifying
   D. subjective
   E. lustrous

4. OPULENT
   A. ostentatious
   B. satiny
   C. desolate
   D. sheer
   E. laconic

Analogies: Select the answer choice that best completes the meaning of the sentence.

5. Grandiose is to lavish as
   A. charade is to false
   B. pretense is to subjective
   C. homage is to loathsome
   D. tribute is to confounding
   E. pretentious is to lustrous

6. Acquisitive is to philanthropic as
   A. greedy is to nefarious
   B. avaricious is to pernicious
   C. covetous is to generous
   D. rapacious is to truculent
   E. solicitous is to histrionic

Sentence Completions: Choose the word that, when inserted in the sentence, <u>best</u> fits the meaning of the sentence as a whole.

7. Explorers in the fifteenth century were motivated as much by desire for adventure as by _____ and the desire to accumulate wealth.
   A. philanthropy
   B. sirens
   C. opulence
   D. acquiescence
   E. avarice

8. Many photographers find the subtlety of black-and-white photos more poignant than the _____ sheen of color photos.
   A. subjective
   B. lustrous
   C. iniquitous
   D. compliant
   E. ebony

1. **A.** *Confound* and *perplex* mean *confuse.* *Fret* means *worry, inure* means *desensitize, billow* means *fill with wind,* and *distend* means *swell.*

2. **E.** *Loathsome* means *repulsive. Acquisitive, avaricious, covetous,* and *rapacious* mean *greedy.*

3. **B.** *Ornate* means *adorned. Baffling* and *mystifying* mean *confusing, subjective* means *personal opinion,* and *lustrous* means *shiny.* Something that is ornate might be shiny, but *adorned* is a more direct definition.

4. **A.** *Opulent* and *ostentatious* mean *showy. Satiny* means *shiny, desolate* means *miserable, sheer* means *steep,* and *laconic* means *brief and rude.*

5. **A.** "A grandiose display is lavish."
   - (A.) A charade display is false . . . yes.
   - B . A pretense (false display) display is subjective (personal) . . . not necessarily.
   - C . A homage (honoring) display is loathsome (repulsive) . . . no.
   - D . A tribute (honoring) display is confounding (stumping) . . . no.
   - E . A pretentious (showy) display is lustrous (shiny) . . . not necessarily.

   Choice A is not ideal, but using the process of elimination, it's better than the other choices.

6. **C.** "Acquisitive (greedy) is the opposite of philanthropic (generous)."
   - A . Greedy is the opposite of nefarious (wicked) . . . no.
   - B . Avaricious (greedy) is the opposite of pernicious (wicked) . . . no.
   - (C.) Covetous (greedy) is the opposite of generous . . . yes!
   - D . Rapacious (greedy) is the opposite of truculent (hostile) . . . no.
   - E . Solicitous (concerned) is the opposite of histrionic (dramatic) . . . no.

7. **E.** "Explorers in the fifteenth century were motivated as much by desire for adventure as by <u>greed</u> and the desire to accumulate wealth."

   Avarice (from your word *avaricious*) means *greed.*

8. **B.** "Many photographers find the subtlety of black-and-white photos more poignant than the <u>????</u> sheen of color photos."

   On the rare occasion that you can't think of a word to fill the blank, try the choices and use the process of elimination. *Lustrous,* meaning *shiny,* is clearly the best choice.

Group 39
Stilted Apologies

Find each of the following words on the *New Moon* page number provided. Based on the way each word is used in the book, guess at its definition.

1. **Fleetingly** (p. 488) might mean _____

   _____

2. **Pretense** (p. 491) might mean _____

   _____

3. **Portcullis** (p. 492) might mean _____

   _____

4. **Discord** (p. 497) might mean _____

   _____

5. **Brusque** (p. 497) might mean _____

   _____

6. **Stilted** (p. 497) might mean _____

   _____

7. **Garbled** (p. 498) might mean _____

   _____

8. **Thrum** (p. 498) might mean _____

   _____

162 Let's see how you did. Check your answers, write the exact definitions, and reread the sentence in *New Moon* where each word appears. Then complete the drills on the next page.

1. **Fleetingly** (p. 488) means *temporarily.* That reminds me of *transitory,* meaning *changing* or *impermanent,* from Group 33. Other synonyms for *fleeting:* ephemeral, evanescent, momentary, transient.

2. **Pretense** (p. 491) means *false display.* This was a synonym for *semblance* in Group 23 and *charade* in Group 32. The other synonyms were *facade, farce, guise, hoax, ruse,* and *sham.*

3. **Portcullis** (p. 492) means *large sliding castle gate.* You can see the word part *port-,* which means *door,* is similar to *porte,* which means *door* in French. *Portcullis* is a great word for the GED or SSAT. We've already discussed that these tests like to use nature words; they also like to use a few simple history and architecture words.

4. **Discord** (p. 497) means *conflict* or *lack of harmony. Discord* even sounds like *not being in the right* **chord**—*lack of harmony.* And in fact, the prefix *dis-* means *not* or *lack of.*

5. **Brusque** (p. 497) means *short and rude. Brusque* was a synonym for *abrupt* in Group 19. The other synonyms were *blunt, curt, laconic,* and *terse.*

6. **Stilted** (p. 497) means *awkward* or *strained.* This word actually comes from the **awkward,** ungraceful walk of a person on stilts! Picture it and you'll never forget the meaning of the word *stilted.*

7. **Garbled** (p. 498) means *distorted.* If you had **marbles** in your mouth, your words would sound **garbled.**

8. **Thrum** (p. 498) means *hum,* like the reverberation (echo) of a string **strummed** on a guitar.

Synonyms: Select the word or phrase whose meaning is closest to the word in capital letters.

1. FLEETING
   A. curt
   B. brusque
   C. laconic
   D. transitory
   E. terse

2. PRETENSE
   A. facade
   B. opulence
   C. lavishness
   D. ostentation
   E. furtiveness

3. BRUSQUE
   A. infallible
   B. deferent
   C. compliant
   D. blunt
   E. acquiescing

4. GARBLED
   A. distorted
   B. euphoric
   C. iniquitous
   D. grisly
   E. capacious

Analogies: Select the answer choice that best completes the meaning of the sentence.

5. Interminable is to fleeting as
   A. transient is to ephemeral
   B. relentless is to leader
   C. eternal is to evanescent
   D. garbled is to chasm
   E. stilted is to momentary

6. Portcullis is to antechamber as
   A. turret is to archer
   B. castle is to moat
   C. knight is to vampire
   D. Edward is to Felix
   E. antechamber is to main room

Sentence Completions: Choose the word that, when inserted in the sentence, <u>best</u> fits the meaning of the sentence as a whole.

7. Watching the _____ between Rosaline and Edward can sometimes be upsetting, making one wish they got along more smoothly.
   A. hoax
   B. ruse
   C. portcullis
   D. thrum
   E. discord

8. Ngo and Joica had been best friends long enough that even a fight did not _____ the solid foundation of their friendship.
   A. discord
   B. confound
   C. stilt
   D. inure
   E. palliate

1. **D.** *Fleeting* and *transitory* mean *temporary*. *Curt, brusque, laconic,* and *terse* mean *brief and rude*. These words describe communication that is **brief** and are related to *temporary,* but are not as direct a definition as *transitory*.

2. **A.** *Pretense* and *facade* mean *false display*. *Opulence, lavishness,* and *ostentation* mean *showiness*. *Furtiveness* means *secretiveness*.

3. **D.** *Brusque* and *blunt* mean *brief. Infallible* means *flawless;* and *deferent, compliant,* and *acquiescing* mean *respectful*.

4. **A.** *Garbled* means *distorted*. *Euphoric* means *very excited, iniquitous* means *wicked, grisly* means *unpleasant,* and *capacious* means *spacious*.

5. **C.** "Interminable (unending) is the opposite of fleeting (temporary)."
   A. Transient (temporary) is the opposite of ephemeral (temporary) . . . no.
   B. Relentless (unending) is the opposite of leader . . . no.
   C. Eternal (unending) is the opposite of evanescent (temporary) . . . yes.
   D. Garbled (distorted) is the opposite of chasm (deep pit) . . . no.
   E. Stilted (awkward) is the opposite of momentary (temporary) . . . no.

6. **E.** "A portcullis is the gate before the antechamber (entry room)."
   A. A turret is the gate before the archer . . . no.
   B. A castle is the gate before the moat . . . no, maybe the other way around.
   C. A knight is the gate before the vampire . . . no.
   D. Edward is the gate before the Felix . . . no, and I know you only chose this one because it said Edward!
   E. An antechamber is the gate before the main room . . . maybe. Using the process of elimination, choice E is best.

7. **E.** "Watching the _not getting along_ between Rosaline and Edward can sometimes be upsetting, making one wish they got along more smoothly."
   Discord means *tension* or *lack of harmony*.

8. **C.** "Ngo and Joica had been best friends long enough that even a fight did not _hurt_ the solid foundation of their friendship."
   Stilt means *strain*. Watch out for choice A, a "fight" might cause *discord,* but *discord* does not fit the flow of the sentence. That's why you think of a word for the blank *before* looking at the choices.

Group 40
Epiphany!

Find each of the following words on the *New Moon* page number provided.
Based on the way each word is used in the book, guess at its definition.

1. **Genteel** (p. 500) might mean _____

   _____

2. **Civility** (p. 500) might mean _____

   _____

3. **Misapprehension** (p. 509) might mean _____

   _____

4. **Blasphemy** (p. 510) might mean _____

   _____

5. **Objective** (p. 513) might mean _____

   _____

6. **Compatible** (p. 516) might mean _____

   _____

7. **Epiphany** (p. 526) might mean _____

   _____

8. **Undermine** (p. 544) might mean _____

   _____

Let's see how you did. Check your answers, write the exact definitions, and reread the sentence in *New Moon* where each word appears. Then complete the drills on the next page.

1. **Genteel** (p. 500) means *polished and pretentious* (showy). A related SAT, ACT, GED, and SSAT word, *urbane,* means *polished,* but without the pretense. Demetri is **genteel,** while Carlisle is **urbane.** Synonym: decorous.

2. **Civility** (p. 500) means *politeness.*

3. **Misapprehension** (p. 509) means *misunderstanding.* That definition makes sense since *mis-* means *wrong* or *bad,* as in *mistake* and *misstep,* and *apprehension* can mean *understanding.*

4. **Blasphemy** (p. 510) means *speaking wrongly about holy things.* This is a beautiful use of the word; Edward sees his relationship with Bella as holy, so when he lied about it in an attempt to protect her, he was *speaking wrongly about something holy.* Synonym: profanity.

5. **Objective** (p. 513) means *scientific, not influenced by personal opinions.* It is defined in the word that follows it in *New Moon,* "clinical," meaning *scientific. Objective* is the opposite of the word *subjective* from Group 38.

6. **Compatible** (p. 516) means *matching.* This word is often used to describe couples that fit together well.

7. **Epiphany** (p. 526) means *major insight.* Okay, you're back in your dream English class with a reading-comprehension question. What is Bella's epiphany? Hint: Always read before and after the line to find the answer to a reading-comprehension question—it's on the next page. Got it? Okay, now please pass the tissues.

8. **Undermine** (p. 544) means *weaken*—if someone **mines underneath** a building, it **weakens** the foundation of the building. The SAT, ACT, GED, and SSAT absolutely love using this word. I bet it will be on your test!

Synonyms: Select the word or phrase whose meaning is closest to the word in capital letters.

1. GENTEEL
   A. decorous
   B. nebulous
   C. fleeting
   D. laconic
   E. stilted

2. OBJECTIVE
   A. subjective
   B. urbane
   C. blasphemous
   D. relenting
   E. clinical

3. EPIPHANY
   A. misapprehension
   B. pretense
   C. ruse
   D. insight
   E. sham

4. UNDERMINE
   A. weaken
   B. garble
   C. cease
   D. confound
   E. fret

Analogies: Select the answer choice that best completes the meaning of the sentence.

5. Objective is to subjective as
   A. adorned is to ornamented
   B. opulent is to ostentatious
   C. scientific is to personal
   D. acquisitive is to covetous
   E. acquiescence is to submission

6. Compatible is to corresponding as
   A. blasphemy is to profanity
   B. civility is to irreverence
   C. discord is to thrum
   D. lustrous is to dull
   E. microscopic is to capacious

Sentence Completions: Choose the word that, when inserted in the sentence, <u>best</u> fits the meaning of the sentence as a whole.

7. Jasmine was known for her _____ in all situations, even ones that tested her urbane nature.
   A. transgression
   B. belligerence
   C. truculence
   D. civility
   E. petulance

8. An imminent blizzard _____ the train's attempts to stay on schedule, delaying it nearly one hour.
   A. severed
   B. goaded
   C. lurched
   D. infused
   E. undermined

1. **A.** *Genteel* and *decorous* mean *polished but showy. Nebulous* means *unclear, fleeting* means *temporary, laconic* means *brief but rude,* and *stilted* means *awkward.*

2. **E.** *Objective* and *clinical* mean *scientific.* Choice A, the word *subjective,* is the opposite. *Urbane* means *polished but without pretense, blasphemous* means *speaking wrongly about something holy,* and *relenting* means *giving in.*

3. **D.** *Epiphany* means *insight. Misapprehension* means *misunderstanding. Pretense, ruse,* and *sham* mean *false display.*

4. **A.** *Undermine* means *weaken. Garble* means *distort, cease* means *end, confound* means *stump,* and *fret* means *worry.*

5. **C.** "Objective (scientific) is the opposite of subjective (personal)."
   - A . Adorned (decorated) is the opposite of ornamented . . . no.
   - B . Opulent (decorated) is the opposite of ostentatious (showy) . . . no.
   - C. Scientific is the opposite of personal . . . yes!
   - D. Acquisitive (greedy) is the opposite of covetous (greedy) . . . no.
   - E . Acquiescence (giving in) is the opposite of submission (giving in) . . . no.

6. **A.** "Compatible means corresponding."
   - A. Blasphemy (profanity) means profanity . . . yes!
   - B . Civility (politeness) means irreverence (rudeness) . . . no.
   - C . Discord (disharmony) means thrum (hum) . . . no.
   - D . Lustrous (shiny) means dull . . . no.
   - E . Microscopic (tiny) means capacious (spacious) . . . no.

7. **D.** "Jasmine was known for her *urbanity/politeness* in all situations, even ones that tested her urbane nature."
   Civility means *politeness. Transgression* means *rule-breaking, belligerence* and *truculence* mean *hostility and aggressiveness,* and *petulance* means *irritability.*

8. **E.** "An imminent blizzard *delayed* the train's attempts to stay on schedule, delaying it nearly one hour."
   Undermined means *weakened* and fits best.

Quiz 8

I. Let's review some of the words that you've seen in Groups 36–40. Match each of the following words to the correct definition or synonym on the right. Then check the solutions on page 172.

1. Subterranean	A. Capacious
2. Contemptuous	B. Desensitize
3. Cavernous	C. Avaricious
4. Inure	D. Compliance
5. Baleful	E. Underground
6. Deference	F. Disobedient
7. Acquisitive	G. Ruse
8. Subjective	H. Malicious
9. Opulent	I. Decorous
10. Fleeting	J. Weaken
11. Pretense	K. Clinical
12. Brusque	L. Personal
13. Genteel	M. Grandiose
14. Objective	N. Terse
15. Undermine	O. Evanescent

II. Let's review several of the word parts that you've seen in Groups 36–40. Match each of the following word parts to the correct definition or synonym on the right. Then check the solutions on page 172.

16. Sub-	A. Earth
17. Terra-	B. Wrong, bad
18. Ante-	C. Under, below
19. Mis-	D. Characterized by
20. -ous	E. Door
21. Port-	F. Before

Review

Match each group of synonyms to its general meaning. Then check the solutions on page 172.

1. Alleviate
   Ameliorate
   Appease
   Assuage
   Conciliate
   Pacify
   Palliate
   Placate

   A. Graceful

2. Facade
   Guise
   Pretense
   Semblance

   B. Little

3. Adept
   Adroit
   Agile
   Deft
   Dexterous
   Lithe
   Nimble
   Supple

   C. Shy, fearful

4. Apprehensive
   Diffident
   Pusillanimous
   Timid
   Timorous

   D. Soothe

5. Exiguous
   Inadequate
   Meager
   Negligible
   Paltry
   Scant

   E. False appearance

Quiz and Review Solutions

Quiz 1	Quiz 2	Quiz 3	Quiz 4	Groups 1–20 Review
1. E	1. E	1. D	1. D	1. D
2. A	2. A	2. A	2. A	2. E
3. F	3. F	3. F	3. E	3. A
4. B	4. B	4. B	4. B	4. F
5. H	5. G	5. I	5. H	5. C
6. C	6. C	6. C	6. C	6. B
7. D	7. K	7. G	7. F	
8. J	8. D	8. E	8. J	
9. I	9. H	9. H	9. G	
10. G	10. L	10. O	10. O	
11. O	11. N	11. N	11. N	
12. K	12. O	12. J	12. I	
13. N	13. I	13. L	13. K	
14. M	14. M	14. M	14. L	
15. L	15. J	15. K	15. M	
16. B	16. B or F	16. D	16. C	
17. D	17. C	17. F	17. D	
18. E	18. D	18. B	18. F	
19. A	19. A	19. A	19. A	
20. F	20. B or F	20. C	20. B	
21. C	21. E	21. E	21. E	

Quiz and Review Solutions

Quiz 5	Quiz 6	Quiz 7	Quiz 8	Groups 21–40 Review
1. E	1. D	1. E	1. E	1. D
2. A	2. A	2. D	2. F	2. E
3. D	3. F	3. F	3. A	3. A
4. B	4. B	4. B	4. B	4. C
5. F	5. H	5. I	5. H	5. B
6. H	6. E	6. A	6. D	
7. J	7. C	7. C	7. C	
8. C	8. K	8. K	8. L	
9. L	9. L	9. M	9. M	
10. M	10. G	10. G	10. O	
11. G	11. O	11. O	11. G	
12. O	12. N	12. H	12. N	
13. N	13. I	13. N	13. I	
14. I	14. J	14. L	14. K	
15. K	15. M	15. J	15. J	
16. D	16. C	16. D	16. C	
17. F	17. E	17. A	17. A	
18. A	18. A	18. E	18. F	
19. B	19. F	19. F	19. B	
20. C or E	20. B	20. B	20. D	
21. C or E	21. D	21. C	21. E	

Answer to Group 27 quiz question: Daniel Cudmore, who plays the Volturi Felix.

Glossary

Aberrant abnormal. Synonyms: *anomalous, atypical, deviant, divergent*

Abrupt brief and rude. Synonyms: *blunt, brusque, curt, laconic, terse*

Absolute total. Synonyms: *consummate, unconditional, unequivocal, unmitigated, unqualified, untempered*

Abstruse puzzling

Abyss deep or bottomless pit. Synonyms: *chasm, void*

Acquisitive curious, greedy. Synonyms: *avaricious, covetous, rapacious*

Adept able, skilled

Affably in a friendly way. Synonyms: *amiably, congenially, genially*

Aghast horrified

Agilely gracefully. Synonyms for agile: *adept, adroit, deft, dexterous, lithe, nimble, supple*

Albino a person with white skin and hair

Allegiance loyalty. Synonym: *fidelity*

Aloof distant

Androgynous not appearing clearly male or female

Annihilating completely destroying. Synonyms: *eradicating, obliterating*

Antagonism hostility. Synonyms: *acrimony, animosity, animus, antipathy, enmity, rancor*

Antechamber entry room that precedes a larger room

Antisocial not social or solitary

Aplomb calm self-confidence

Apt appropriate, likely, or able. Synonyms: *apposite, apropos, germane, pertinent*

Articulation clear pronunciation

Ascertain find out for sure

Atone make amends or pay back. Synonyms: *expiate, recompense, redress*

Attuned in tune with

Authoritative with authority or commanding

Avenge get revenge

Aversion avoidance or intense dislike. Synonyms: *animosity, antipathy, disinclination, enmity*

Aviary a place where birds are kept

Baleful threatening. Synonyms: *depraved, heinous, impious, iniquitous, malevolent, malicious, menacing, nefarious, pernicious, sinister*

Bane burden or curse

Banter joke back and forth. Synonyms: *badinage, raillery, repartee*

Basilisk a legendary giant serpent with a deadly stare

Belligerent hostile and aggressive. Synonyms: *bellicose, pugnacious, truculent*

Bibliophile a person who loves books

Bile anger. Synonym: *vitriol*

Billowed filled with air

Blanched paled or turned white

Blasphemy speaking wrongly about holy things. Synonym: *profanity*

Blithely with insensitive cheerfulness

Bough tree branch

Brawny strong and muscular. Synonym: *burly*

Brevity shortness

Brittle fragile or breakable

Brooding unhappily

Brusque short and rude. Synonyms: *abrupt, blunt, curt, laconic, terse*

Buffeting battering

Callous insensitive

Canine dog-like

Capitulation surrender. Synonyms for capitulate: *cede, concede, relent, yield*

Carcasses dead animal bodies

Carnage slaughter or massacre

Castanets small, shell-shaped percussion instruments

Cataclysmic disastrous. Synonyms: *calamitous, catastrophic, dire*

Cavernous very spacious. Synonyms: *capacious, voluminous*

Ceasing stopping

Cerebral mental, brainy

Chafing becoming annoyed or irritated

Charade false display. Synonyms: *facade, farce, hoax, pretense, ruse, sham*

Chastised scolded. Synonyms: *admonished, censured, rebuked, reprimanded, reproached, reproved*

Civility politeness

Clinically scientifically or without emotion

Coalescing coming together. Synonyms: *amalgamating, converging, fusing, homogenizing*

Coaxed urged or persuaded. Synonyms for coax: *cajole, enjoin, entreat, exhort, goad, implore, incite, prod, spur*

Comity a group of nations

Commingle mix together

Commiserate feel sympathy with

Communism a political philosophy in which all property is publicly owned

Compatible matching

Compelled required

Compendious information grouped together in a short, but complete way

Composure calmness. Synonyms: *aplomb, equanimity, poise, sangfroid, serenity, tranquility*

Compulsion obsession

Compunctions regrets. Synonyms: *contrition, penitence, qualms, repentance, remorse, ruefulness, scruples*

Confidant trusted friend or ally

Confide tell the truth to or trust

Confounds stumps. Synonyms: *baffles, mystifies, perplexes*

Congealing coming together. Synonyms: *amalgamating, coalescing, converging, fusing, homogenizing*

Conspiratorially plotting together. Synonyms for conspire: *collude, machinate, subterfuge*

Contemptuous angry and disobedient. Synonyms for contempt: *abhorrence, derision, disdain, scorn*

Contingency possibility. Synonym: *eventuality*

Contorting twisting or knotting up

Convalescence recovery. Synonym: *recuperation*

Conviction sureness, or a jury's pronouncement of guilt. Synonym: *certitude*

Corpses dead human bodies

Corresponding matching

Coven group of vampires (or witches)

Cowered hid fearfully

Crescent half-moon–shaped. Synonyms: *lunette, lunula*

Crimson purplish-red

Curriculum plan of study

Deference giving in and showing respect. Synonyms: *acquiescence, compliance, obeisance, submission*

Defiled contaminated.
Synonyms: *befouled, marred, sullied, tainted*

Deity god or goddess

Desolate miserable or deserted

Devoid empty

Dilapidated run-down.
Synonyms: *decrepit, ramshackle*

Dire dangerous or serious

Discord conflict or lack of harmony

Dismissively showing that something does not matter

Distended stretched or swollen.
Synonyms: *bloated, engorged, protuberant*

Dithering being indecisive.
Synonyms: *vacillating, wavering*

Divert steer away or entertain

Ebony black

Ecstatic very excited. Synonyms: *buoyant, ebullient, elated, euphoric, exuberant, exultant, jubilant, rapturous*

Eddies swirls of water or wind

Edict formal declaration.
Synonyms: *decree, fiat, mandate, proclamation*

Edifice building

Eerie spooky

Egregious very bad

Elated very psyched. Synonyms: *buoyant, ebullient, ecstatic, euphoric, exuberant, exultant, jubilant, and rapturous*

Elusive hard to find or hold on to. Synonyms: *equivocal, evasive, indefinable*

En masse grouped together

Entail involve

Entourage the people around a famous or important person.
Synonyms: *attendants, posse, retainers, retinue*

Epiphany major insight

Equivocal unclear

Eternity very long or endless time. Synonym: *perpetuity*

Exasperation irritation

Excising removing

Exposition back-story or explanation

Extraordinarily very

Exuberant very excited.
Synonyms: *buoyant, ebullient, ecstatic, elated, euphoric, exultant, jubilant, rapturous*

Exultant very excited.
Synonyms: *buoyant, ebullient, ecstatic, elated, euphoric, exuberant, jubilant, rapturous*

Faux pas violation of social rules

Festering getting much worse

Fickle unreliable or changing too easily. Synonyms: *capricious, erratic, mercurial, vacillating*

Fleetingly temporarily. Synonyms for fleeting: *ephemeral, evanescent, impermanent, momentary, transient, transitory*

Flout disobey or disregard

Foiled defeated. Synonyms: *stymied, thwarted*

Foremost leading

Foresight seeing into the future. Synonyms: *foreboding, intuition, premonition, presentiment*

Formidable very powerful

Fret worry

Furtively secretly. Synonyms: *clandestinely, covertly, stealthily, surreptitiously*

Garbled distorted

Genteel polished and pretentious (showy). Synonym: *decorous*

Ghoulish disturbing and unpleasant. Synonyms: *ghastly, grisly, grotesque, macabre, morbid*

Glacial icy

Glum sad. Synonyms: *despondent (very glum), gloomy, morose, pessimistic, sullen*

Goaded urged. Synonyms: *cajoled, coaxed, enjoined, entreated, exhorted, implored, incited, prodded, spurred*

Grating harsh. Synonym: *strident*

Grimace an expression of pain or disgust

Grotesque very disgusting

Gruesome horrible. Synonyms: *grisly, grotesque*

Haggard tired and unhealthy looking

Heady very powerful, intoxicating, thrilling, or cerebral

Histrionic dramatic

Homogenizing making all of something the same (uniform)

Humongous huge. Synonyms: *colossal, enormous, gargantuan, gigantic, immense, mammoth, monstrous*

Hysteria panic or intense emotion

Imminent occurring soon. Synonyms: *forthcoming, impending, looming*

Impaired weakened

Impasse dead end. Synonyms: *deadlock, stalemate*

Impassive not feeling or showing emotion. Synonym: *inscrutable*

Impending looming or about to happen. Synonym: *imminent*

Imperious commanding, bossy

Impish playful or mischievous

Implications hinted meanings

Implored begged

Impulsive on an impulse or spontaneous. Synonyms: *hasty, impetuous, rash, unpremeditated*

Incisors sharp teeth

Indecipherable not readable or not understandable. Synonym: *inscrutable*

Indifferently without concern or interest. Synonyms: *apathetic, dispassionate, nonchalant*

Ineptly without skill

Inevitable unavoidable. Synonym: *inexorable*

Inexorably unstoppably

Infallible always right

Infectious contagious. Synonyms: *communicable, transferable, transmittable*

Infiltrated entered

Infuse mix

Injunction formal order. Synonyms: *decree, dictum, directive, edict, fiat, mandate, proclamation, writ*

Interminable endless. Synonyms: *ceaseless, eternal, incessant, perpetual, relentless, unremitting*

Intermittently on and off, sporadically

Interspersed scattered or dispersed among

Intonation pitch. Synonyms: *cadence, inflection, timber*

Intrigued curious or interested

Intrusive invasive

Inure hold back. Synonym: *desensitize*

Irate furious. Synonyms: *incensed, infuriated, livid*

Ironic happening in a different and disappointingly funnier way than expected

Jade green with a bluish tint

Kismet fate

Lapse failure or mistake

Leer an unpleasant or even hostile look, or an inappropriately lustful look. Synonyms: *ogle, sneer*

Listlessly with no energy. Synonyms for listless: *exhausted, lethargic, sluggish, weary, with lassitude, with torpor*

Livid furious. Synonyms: *incensed, infuriated, irate*

Loathsome repulsive or hateable

Loitered hung around

Loped ran or jogged with a graceful stride

Lupine wolf-like

Lurched jerked or staggered

Lustrous shiny. Synonyms: *glossy, satiny*

Macabre bloody, deathly, or gruesome. Synonyms: *ghastly, gory, morbid*

Malevolent very hostile or wanting to harm. Synonyms: *abominable, baleful, execrable, loathsome, maleficent, malicious, odious, rancorous, venomous*

Malicious very hostile or wanting to harm. Synonyms: *abominable, baleful, execrable, loathsome, maleficent, malevolent, odious, rancorous, venomous*

Mammoth huge. Synonyms: *colossal, enormous, gargantuan, gigantic, immense, monstrous*

Marveling with amazement

Masochistic enjoying or seeking pain

Mavericks people who do not follow societies' rules. Synonyms: *dissenters, dissidents, nonconformists*

Mayhem disorder (often violent). Synonyms: *anarchy, bedlam, chaos, pandemonium, turmoil*

Meddling interfering

Melodramatic very dramatic. Synonyms: *histrionic, operatic*

Metamorphosis change

Metaphorically symbolically

Microscopic very small

Millennia thousands of years

Mimic imitate. Synonym: *ape*

Misapprehension misunderstanding

Mollified soothed. Synonyms: *alleviate, ameliorate, assuage, conciliate, pacify, palliate, placate*

Monotone a flat, dull tone

Moot irrelevant or uncertain

Moroseness gloominess. Synonyms for morose: *doleful, dour, glum, lugubrious, melancholic, sullen*

Mundane ordinary

Mutated genetically changed

Mystification confusion

Mythical legendary

Nebulous unclear. Synonyms: *ambiguous, amorphous, imprecise, muddled, tenuous, vague*

Objective scientific, not influenced by personal opinions

Oblivion unconsciousness, death, or extinction

Obscure unclear or difficult to understand. Synonyms: *abstruse (puzzling), recondite*

Opulent luxurious and showy. Synonyms: *grandiose, lavish, ostentatious, pretentious, sumptuous*

Ornate decorated in a fancy way. Synonyms: *adorned, elaborate, ornamented*

Ostracism being excluded

Overt obvious. Synonyms: *blatant, evident, manifest, patent*

Parched very dry or very thirsty. Synonyms: *arid, dehydrated, desiccated*

Pathetic pitiful or deserving pity

Perforated pierced or with holes

Perk benefit

Perplexity confusion

Perquisite benefit

Petulance irritability. Synonyms: *peevishness, sullenness*

Philanthropist a person who loves humans and donates money to help charities

Philosophy the study of knowledge

Piqued irritated or hurt, stimulated. Synonyms: *affronted, slighted*

Placate soothe. Synonyms: *alleviate, ameliorate, appease, assuage, conciliate, mollify, pacify, palliate*

Portcullis large sliding castle gate

Potency strength

Precipice cliff. Synonyms: *bluff, crag, escarpment, scarp*

Prehistoric very, very old

Prelude introduction. Synonyms: *commencement, overture, precursor*

Premonition feeling that something bad will happen. Synonyms: *foreboding, intuition, presentiment*

Prescient to know beforehand; to predict

Pretense false display. Synonyms: *charade, facade, farce, guise, hoax, ruse, semblance, sham*

Pretentious showy

Prodded urged. Synonyms for prod: *coax, enjoin, entreat, exhort, goad, implore, incite, spur*

Prolonged unusually long. Synonym: *protracted*

Prominent noticeable or important

Prophetic predicting something. Synonyms: *prescient, visionary*

Protocol code of behavior. Synonym: *convention, decorum, etiquette, propriety*

Pusillanimous timid

Quantifiable measurable

Quarry something hunted or pursued, or a pit where gold or other minerals are mined. Synonym: *prey*

Raking searching, gathering with a rake, setting a stage floor at an angle, or moving in a sweeping motion

Ramshackle run-down. Synonyms: *decrepit, dilapidated*

Rapt fascinated. Synonyms: *captivated, enthralled, mesmerized, riveted*

Ravenous very hungry. Synonyms: *famished, gluttonous, insatiable, rapacious, voracious*

Rebuked scolded strongly. Synonyms: *admonished, censured, chastised, reprimanded, reproached, reproved*

Reciprocate give back. Synonym: *requite*

Reeling staggering or bewildered

Relentless endless or constant. Synonyms: *ceaseless, incessant*

Remnants leftovers

Remorse regret. Synonyms: *compunction, contrition, penitence, repentance, ruefulness*

Remote far away

Reparable repairable. Synonyms: *rectifiable, salvageable*

Reserved holding back or not showing one's feelings. Synonyms: *aloof, introverted, reticent, taciturn*

Reverberated echoed

Reverie thoughts or daydreaming

Running amuck being out of control

Sadistic intentionally cruel

Sallow pale. Synonyms: *alabaster, ashen, blanched, pallid, wan*

Sangfroid excessive composure under danger

Sardonic sarcastic

Scant little. Synonyms: *exiguous, inadequate, meager, negligible, paltry*

Scourge problem or plague. Synonyms: *affliction, bane*

Scrounge dig

Secluded out of the way or sheltered

Semblance appearance. Synonyms: *facade, guise, pretense*

Serpentine winding

Serrated jagged

Severe harsh. Synonym: *stern*

Severed broken or cut apart

Sheer very steep, absolute, or very thin

Shrewdly wisely. Synonyms: *astutely, cannily, cunningly, perspicaciously, sagaciously*

Sienna yellowish-brown or reddish-brown

Sieve literally a strainer, and figuratively a person who forgets easily

Sinister wicked. Synonyms: *baleful, depraved, heinous, impious, iniquitous, malevolent, menacing, nefarious, pernicious*

Siren alluring, but dangerous

Smirking smiling in an annoying way

Solemnly seriously. Synonyms: *earnestly, gravely, sincerely, soberly, somberly*

Solicitously with concern or interest

Sophomoric childish

Sporadically occasionally. Synonym: *intermittently*

Stand grouping, being on one's feet, or a table that holds something

Stilted awkward or strained

Stock belief, products carried by a store, or ownership of a business

Stoic not showing emotion. Synonym: *impassive*

Stupor dazed state or unconsciousness. Synonym: *oblivion*

Stymie block or defeat. Synonyms: *foil, thwart*

Subjective dependent on a person's particular view

Subterranean underground

Sultry hot and humid

Supple graceful and flexible. Synonyms: *limber, lissome, lithe, nimble, willowy*

Surreal unreal

Surreptitiously secretly. Synonyms: *clandestinely, covertly, furtively, stealthily*

Synchronization coordination or harmonizing

Taboo forbidden. Synonyms: *illicit, interdicted, prohibited, proscribed*

Tabulated calculated

Tangible touchable or real

Tawny yellowish-brown. Synonyms: *ocher, topaz*

Tempo speed or pace

Tentative hesitant

Tenuous flimsy or unsubstantiated

Throngs crowds

Thrum hum

Thwarted prevented. Synonyms: *foiled, stymied*

Timidly shyly or with fear. Synonyms: *apprehensively, diffidently, pusillanimously, timorously*

Tolerant patient or forgiving. Synonyms: *forbearing, indulgent, lenient*

Toll the ring of a bell

Topographical showing physical features

Torrents large amounts of fast-moving water

Tranquil calm. Synonyms: *pacific, placid, serene*

Transcribe write from one form to another

Transformation change

Transgressors people who go across boundaries—rule-breakers

Transitory changing or impermanent. Synonyms: *ephemeral, evanescent, transient*

Tribute something that honors. Synonyms: *homage, paean*

Trio a group of three

Triumvirate a group of three people holding power

Trivial unimportant

Turret a cylindrical tower on the corner or wall of a castle

Twilight the period after sunset but before darkness

Unabashed unashamed

Uncanny remarkable. Synonym: *extraordinary*

Undermine weaken

Unendurable unbearable. Synonym: *intolerable*

Unperturbed unconcerned

Unrequited not returned. Synonym: *unreciprocated*

Urbane polished

Virtues good qualities. Opposite of virtue: *vice*

Virtuously with goodness or honor. Synonyms for virtue: *rectitude, righteousness*

Vulpine fox-like

Wallow immerse oneself

Wizened wrinkled

Wretched miserable. Synonyms: *desolate, devastated, disconsolate*